Contents

Flying VFR in Marginal Weather

3rd Edition

TAB
PRACTICAL
FLYING SERIES

Flying VFR in Marginal Weather

3rd Edition

Daryl E. Murphy

Distributed by:
Airlife Publishing Ltd.
101 Longden Road, Shrewsbury SY3 9EB, England

Certified flight instructors, FARs, pilot operating handbooks, or various updated communications by entities mentioned in this book, and other entities, may alter or affect the information published.

Any navigation charts or other material resembling navigation charts in this book are supplied as reference material only; they are not for navigation purposes.

THIRD EDITION
FIRST PRINTING

© 1991 by **TAB Books**.
Earlier editions © 1987 and 1980 by TAB Books.
TAB Books is a division of McGraw-Hill, Inc.

Library of Congress Cataloging-in-Publication Data

Murphy, Daryl E.
     Flying VFR in marginal weather / by Daryl E. Murphy.—3rd ed.
          p.   cm.
     Includes index.
     ISBN 0-8306-8699-1   ISBN 0-8306-7699-6 (pbk.)
     1. Airplanes—Piloting.   2. Meteorology in aeronautics.
   I. Title.
TL710.M87   1991
629.132′52—dc20
                                                    91-11322
                                                    CIP

TAB Books offers software for sale. For information and a catalog, please contact
TAB Software Department, Blue Ridge Summit, PA 17294-0850.

Acquisitions Editor: Jeff Worsinger
Book Editor: Suzanne L. Cheatle
Production: Katherine G. Brown
Book Design: Jaclyn J. Boone
Series Design: Jaclyn J. Boone   PFS

Preface

THIS BOOK IS NOT INTENDED TO ENCOURAGE PILOTS TO FLY INTO MARGINAL weather conditions or to take silly chances of any kind. Its purpose, rather, is to demonstrate how such situations can be dealt with when a pilot has inadvertently come face to face with conditions that are beyond the limits of his experience or capabilities or that go beyond the capabilities of the aircraft involved.

All of the examples used in the following pages are based on actual incidents. Any names and aircraft identifications used are fictitious in order to protect those involved. Quite frequently the solutions to a particular problem involve actions by the pilot that might be contrary to the Federal Air Regulations (FARs) and must be looked at as emergency measures. It goes without saying that pilots should, when at all possible, operate within the rules and regulations set forth in the FARs. Still, when faced by what appears to be, at the time, an unavoidable choice, safe is to be selected in preference to legal.

With weather continuing to be the primary cause of accidents among general aviation pilots in general and Visual Flight Rules (VFR) pilots in particular, most of the case histories used in this book are weather-related incidents. But also included are some in which the weather, as such, was not the primary cause of the developing danger.

An uninformed reader might get the impression from what follows that flying light aircraft involves a never-ending series of hair-raising situations in which the pilot and his passengers face nearly insurmountable dangers. That, in fact, is not the case. The average and reasonably proficient pilot can spend thousands of hours at the controls of light aircraft without encountering any serious emergencies. If he is careful and resists the temptation to take unnecessary chances, it is unlikely that he will ever be faced with the need to make a life-and-death decision. However, flying, like most other human activities, involves a certain calculated risk, and it is in an effort to minimize that risk factor that this book has been compiled.

Introduction

W HEN YOU'RE A STUDENT PILOT, YOU GET THE FEELING THAT YOUR instructor considers your intelligence somewhere between that of a rock and a tree because no matter how well you accomplish even the most rudimentary task, you have to keep doing it over and over to prove yourself to your teacher.

Then one day, you rebel against this unquestionable authority by saying something like, "Why do I have to keep doing this stupid exercise? I can do it in my sleep!" And if your instructor was like mine, he'll simply smile and say, "That's right," thereby revealing the Wisdom of Flying: if you do it the same every time, without even thinking, you'll do it without thinking every time.

Flying involves a risk, just like most activities. For some people it's a high risk; for others, a low risk. Low-risk pilots are those who fly within their envelope of capability—able to do both the routine and the exceptional tasks without thinking.

However, the one element that challenges both the high- and low-risk pilot is weather—clouds, fog, wind, turbulence, precipitation, and temperature. Ever-changing, weather presents constant opportunities to the VFR pilot that demand decisions, and the choice might not always be the correct one.

This revised and updated edition of *Flying VFR in Marginal Weather* is presented to help the VFR pilot be better informed about the right decisions when confronted by a "wrong" situation.

1
What Is
Marginal Weather?

TO PARAPHRASE AN OLD AVIATION IDIOM, THERE ARE TWO KINDS OF VFR pilots: those who have broken the rules, and those who haven't . . . yet. Some of the joys of flight—its lack of ordinary physical restraints, its time-saving nature, and its far-ranging freedom—are the very things that may often lure us into that gray area of operation known as *marginal*.

The term *marginal* might mean one thing to a pilot with limited experience and quite another to one who has been flying for years. Generally, *marginal weather* is thought of as a condition of minimal or lowering ceilings and deteriorating visibility, but the description also can involve strong winds; turbulence; precipitation; extremes of heat or cold; excessive flight altitude without on-board oxygen; or smoke, haze, smog, or icing under adverse temperature and/or humid conditions.

TAKING A LOOK

Probably most VFR weather-related accidents are the result of a pilot who wants to take a look to see if the weather conditions are better a bit farther ahead. And it's a terribly tempting curiosity: you're flying along under a 5,000-foot or so overcast, dodging intermittent rain showers and occasional low-hanging scud. Except for the fact that there isn't any turbulence, it's pretty pleasant, and your destination a few hundred miles distant is reporting scattered conditions with good visibility. You figure that sooner or later you ought to be able to get out of this mess.

Following the Interstate

There's this big interstate highway underneath you that is running more or less along your route of flight, so you stay a bit to the right of it in order to be able to comfortably keep it in sight to your left. You figure—with a certain amount of justification—that as long as you can see that highway for a fair distance of a mile or so ahead, you'll be okay (FIG. 1-1).

Suddenly that group of occasionally low-hanging scud turns into something more solid and you drop down lower. For a moment, that highway ahead is gone. Then you see it again, only now you might be just a thousand feet or so above the ground. That's still not too bad, but you kind of hope that it's not going to get much worse.

The cars coming toward you down below have their headlights on, even though it's still several hours before sunset. That should tip you off that the weather farther on is likely to get worse, not better, but it might not occur to you. Suddenly, you realize that the highway doesn't seem to be there anymore; it just disappeared from sight (FIG. 1-2). Within seconds you're in the middle of a rain shower, which makes an incredible racket as it pelts your windscreen. Straight down, you can still see the cars with their headlights on, but ahead there is nothing.

You briefly consider turning back, but figure a shower like that can't last forever. After all, it's only about another 45 minutes until you get to where you want to go, and if the weather information was right about the scattered conditions, you're bound to break into sunshine pretty soon.

On the average, you'll probably make it just fine. You might spend another 20 or 30 minutes being extremely uncomfortable, with damp palms and dripping armpits,

Fig. 1-1. *As long as you can see the highway below, the weather conditions cannot be too bad.*

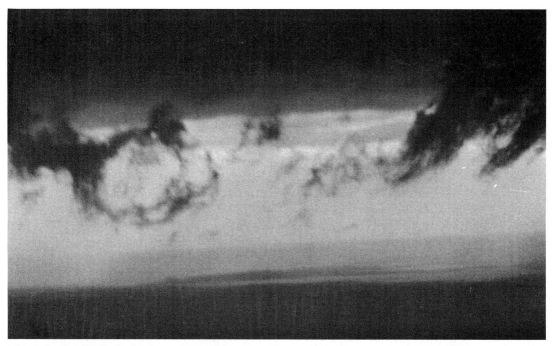

Fig. 1-2. *Suddenly, the highway is not there any more, and conditions are getting worse.*

but by sticking religiously to the highway below and watching your airspeed indicator and altimeter more carefully than usual, you'll likely break out of this mess just before reaching your destination.

Featureless Terrain

But what if there hadn't been that highway (FIG. 1-3)? What if you had been flying over a featureless plain, rolling hills, or the endless woods in southern Georgia and Mississippi? The temptation to fly on and take a look would be just as strong. The reason you're in the air, after all, is that there is some place where you feel you have to be, and that some place is, as always, just beyond the weather ahead.

The difficulty is that you want to keep track of where you are relative to your desired course, while also keeping a sharp eye out for what is happening behind you, just in case you find it necessary to beat a hasty retreat. Most probably there is low-hanging weather all around, but there is something that looks like a light spot more or less in the direction you want to go (FIG. 1-4). So you plow on toward that lighter area, and sure enough, you come to a place where the overcast seems much thinner, but it's a small area, and all the low clouds and showers continue. In all probability, things have closed down behind you and you have no choice but to fly on, staying just as low as the terrain permits. For some time now, you have been unable to receive a VOR,

Fig. 1-3. *What if there is no highway to follow?*

and your nav receiver is tuned to the next station along the route, its OFF flag continuing to tell you that you're still beyond reception distance.

The chances are that you'll be ending up a considerable distance off course without being fully aware of it, and trying to become reoriented strictly by pilotage is extremely difficult under these conditions. Because you are low, the number of features that can be identified is limited, and somehow nothing seems to look the way it should according to the chart. In addition, because you're so close to the ground, the chore of flying the airplane requires your constant attention, making the studying of charts problematical, if not impossible.

Whatever you do, flying the airplane must necessarily take precedence over any other activity. As long as you have the airplane under control and there is ample fuel in the tanks, there is always a way out. Just don't panic. Stay cool and remember, if all else fails and you suddenly find out there is no direction left in which you can continue VFR, your escape route (unless there happens to be a place at which you can land) is up, period.

When VFR pilots let this type of predicament develop into an eventual crash land-

Fig. 1-4. *There is something that looks like a light spot somewhere more or less in the direction you want to go.*

ing—with often catastrophic consequences both for those aboard and the airplane—it is a psychological block that prevents them from accepting the one remaining (albeit illegal) choice—to climb into the overcast to an altitude at which reception can be reestablished. Assuming the always- and all-important ability to control the aircraft by reference to instruments alone, you're then in a position to contact some FSS on the ground and do one of two things: either own up to your predicament and let them guide you to safety at an airport at which the weather is halfway decent, or inquire about the current weather at various locations within your range and then navigate by radio to one that sounds most likely to get you out of the soup in the shortest possible time, even if it means taking a detour or actually retracing your steps.

HIGH-ALTITUDE SITUATIONS

Of course, not all taking-a-look situations take place close to the ground. You might be flying along at a perfectly safe and comfortable altitude, but there, lying smack across your course is a squall line that extends for a considerable distance in either direction. According to the weather reports, it is supposed to be about 20 miles wide, but slightly to your left there is what appears to be a low saddle between the higher buildups. The temptation is to climb up and over that saddle, rather than to accept the delay and extra fuel associated with flying around one end of the squall line or the other.

Most probably at that altitude you're already at full throttle, so you simply trim the nose up and start to climb. As you get closer to the clouds, the likelihood exists that two things will happen at the same time: one is that there will be clouds to the right and left as well as ahead; the other is that the saddle turns out to be higher than you thought. So you steepen your angle of climb, but with clouds obscuring the horizon to either side, you have lost your ability to judge the angle of climb by visual reference to the outside.

Unless your airplane is equipped with an angle-of-attack indicator, the only instrument in the cockpit that is of any value in determining if the angle is getting too steep is the airspeed indicator. The VSI becomes meaningless at an altitude that might be close to the service ceiling of your airplane because the airplane is probably mushing along, showing a rate of climb of only a few hundred feet while it is actually flying at an extreme nose-high attitude. The artificial horizon does show the nose-high condition, but fails to clearly relate it to any reference to the approaching stall. Only the airspeed indicator does that, and when you find that your IAS is getting too low, put the nose down, clouds or no clouds.

Squall Lines

A squall line invariably is made up of thunderstorms, and if you should actually fly into the clouds, your ability to avoid them is reduced to a dangerous level. Therefore, if you can't get up high enough to get over the top of that saddle, turn away from the clouds. If you're still climbing at least 100 fpm or better, you might fly one or several 360s—shallow, because a steep bank will reduce your ability to climb—until you're certain that you can see across the saddle and into what's beyond.

Because you have no visual reference to the horizon, you have no certain way of knowing whether you are looking up, down, or straight ahead; it is a good idea to level the airplane using the artificial horizon. Then, when it's in a level attitude, point the nose toward the saddle and look straight ahead. If the lowest point of the saddle is above the nose of the airplane, you're still too low. If it's level with the nose, it would still be a good idea to climb another few hundred feet. If it's below the nose, what do you see beyond? If the clouds are clearly at the level of the saddle or lower, it is probably all right to fly over it and continue on. But unless you can see with reasonable certainty that you'll be able to get through and continue on for the entire width of the squall line, you'd be a lot better advised to turn back and forget the whole thing.

Always remember that you're probably already as high as your airplane is going to climb, so getting over still-higher cloud tops ahead might no longer be possible. Also, you're likely to be at oxygen altitudes without oxygen in the airplane, and while you might feel perfectly fine and capable of efficiently handling the controls, this in fact might not be the case. Once you have taken the step and flown past that saddle, you're committed to staying at that altitude until you're clear of the squall line. With headwinds at those altitudes often reaching 40 or 50 knots, this could possibly take a while.

Mountainous Terrain

A similar situation often occurs in the mountains. There is an overcast, and many of the mountaintops are obscured by clouds, but the visibility below the clouds is pretty good. You're flying along a valley or across a high plain toward a ridge that extends across your flight path, and most of the tops extend into the base of the clouds. But there is a pass where there appears to be ample space to fly through while staying safely VFR. Here, too, you should be level at an altitude above the base of the pass before actually entering it. The reason is the same as described for squall lines: you have to be able to see what lies beyond. Is there a valley on the other side, is it safely VFR, and once having reached the other side of that valley, will you be able to continue?

Some of this information can be obtained by studying Sectionals. If you know which pass you're looking at (and that is by no means always the case), you can determine from the chart what lies ahead. If the ground falls off on the far side of the pass and there is no second mountain ridge to be crossed, then it's probably reasonably safe to fly through the pass without first making a special effort to see what's beyond.

If, however, you're not sure which pass this is or if the chart shows that there are more mountains ahead, you should enter the pass only with the clear advance decision to make a 180 as soon as there is an indication that continuing VFR on course might become difficult or impossible.

That last-resort escape route, climbing up into the overcast and to a safe altitude, might not work in places like the Rockies, however, where many mountains are higher than the service ceiling of many light aircraft, and clouds are bad enough, but clouds full of rocks could easily spoil your whole day. See chapter 6 for more information on flying in the mountains.

It would be foolish to say here that you should never, under any circumstances, fly into questionable weather conditions in order to take a look. It would probably be a good rule, but it just isn't realistic. Sooner or later, all of us are likely to do it. But there should be two hard and fast prerequisites, without which it should never be attempted.

First, the pilot must be able to control his airplane by means of instruments alone—not only straight and level flight, but in turns, climbs, and descents. Second, there must be plenty of fuel in the tanks. Taking a look means not knowing what is likely to come next and thus, not knowing how long you might need to continue to fly. Too little fuel turns a calculated risk into a foolish chance.

2
Ceilings and Their Limits

THE MINIMUM FOR LEGAL FLIGHT IN CONTROLLED AIRSPACE IS 1,000 FEET from the ground to the base of the clouds. In uncontrolled airspace there is no minimum—the rules simply require the pilot to stay clear of clouds. Technically a *ceiling* is the height above ground level of the lowest layer of clouds, described as either broken or overcast, but not classified as thin, obscured, or partially obscured.

Once a pilot has left the airport traffic area, it is up to him to decide whether conditions along the proposed flight route will continue to be adequately safe for the remainder of the flight.

In flat country, it might be perfectly possible and quite safe to fly long distances under a 1,000-foot ceiling, assuming that the pilot is aware of towers or other man-made obstacles, and that he remembers that whenever he is about to overfly an area located within a 5-mile radius of a controlled airport (30-mile radius of Terminal Control Area), the tower must be contacted to obtain permission to pass through the airport traffic area.

This type of flying is not particularly comfortable and frequently results in pilots flying into a box from which they find it hard to extricate themselves.

VFR ON TOP

One of the all-time favorite means by which VFR pilots avoid low-altitude and/or low-ceiling flight is to go VFR on top. It's also a popular way to get in trouble.

Fig. 2-1. *It's smooth and sunny above the weather.*

See if this sounds familiar: the reason to go on top is simple and quite easy to understand. You take off from an airport with a broken ceiling at 2,000 or 3,000 feet, and it's bumpy and ugly and you get bounced around, yet above and between the broken clouds you know that there is that gorgeous blue sky begging you to shove the throttle in, haul back, and start climbing.

And that's what you do. You weave back and forth to stay clear of the clouds, which are soon rushing by you on either side, and then it's suddenly smooth and a few minutes later you're above all that mess (FIG. 2-1). You sit back, take a deep breath, relax, and say to yourself, "This is what flying is all about!" It's marvelous, comfortable, cool. The true airspeed is higher than it was down below, and the fuel consumption is lower, with the mixture adjusted to just barely on the rich side of peak.

Then you notice—or more likely, don't notice—that the breaks in the undercast gradually get smaller and smaller, until after awhile, there aren't any breaks. Okay . . . as long as there's plenty of fuel in the tanks, you figure there is bound to be a place somewhere between here and your destination where you'll be able to (legally) get down.

Now you spot some higher buildups of clouds sticking up out of the top of the undercast ahead, and you notice that the distance between your flight altitude and the top of the undercast is gradually diminishing (FIG. 2-2). But there's still quite a few thousand feet before you might have to start worrying about oxygen, so you trim the nose up a bit and maybe increase the manifold pressure—if you're not already at full throttle. You watch the altimeter move slowly upward while you manage to stay above those white billows below.

By now it's been a couple of hours since you've actually seen the ground. You've been navigating by radio and might have found that, despite the increase in true air-

Fig. 2-2. *Now you spot some higher buildups sticking out of the undercast ahead.*

speed, your ground speed has deteriorated somewhat, indicating that you must be fighting a fair headwind at these higher altitudes.

The fuel gauges show half for both tanks, so that's not yet a problem. Still, there's a little voice in the back of your head that keeps saying, "One of these days we're going to have to start thinking in terms of getting down from here."

You start to pay closer attention to the weather sequences, and find that most stations along your route are reporting solid overcast conditions, although the ceilings are ample and there is no visibility restriction to speak of.

Options

You're now beginning to think about your available options. Let's say you're at 10,500 feet mean sea level (msl) and somewhere over western Kansas, where the terrain is level with no mountains to worry about, and according to your Sectional, a ground elevation of around 2,000 feet. According to the last weather reports you heard, the ceilings average 4,000 feet, which puts them at 6,000 msl. Your best guess is that the undercast is about 1,000 feet below you, which puts it at 9,000 feet or so, indicating that the clouds are about 3,000 feet thick. At a rate of descent of 500 feet per minute (fpm), this means that it will take about six minutes to get through them—if that turns out to be your only option.

Well, it's still too early to worry about it; you still have sufficient fuel for another 200 or so miles, and you figure that there is bound to be a hole along here somewhere. As a matter of fact, the last weather sequence did include some reports of broken conditions somewhere about 150 miles to the left of your intended course. Should you turn left and suffer the consequences of a detour, or should you take a chance, stay on course, and hope for the best? Maybe if you climb still higher you could spot some of those dark patches in the clouds below that usually indicate thin spots or actual breaks. Why not? Let's try it and see.

When level at 12,500, you do believe that what you see ahead and to the right is a patch of darker clouds, and you head toward it to determine if there are breaks. But, by doing this you have effectively eliminated your option of an escape route to the area of reported broken conditions because it will be beyond the range of your remaining fuel.

It seems to take forever to reach that dark patch of clouds you're aiming for, and you find that your eyes move with increasing frequency to the fuel gauges, which are now around the one-quarter mark, meaning that it won't be very much longer until the choice of action is reduced to one: get down.

If those dark patches in the clouds actually did turn out to be what you hoped they would, you are indeed in luck. Let's say it wasn't an actual hole, but at least a thin spot, which gives you the impression that you can see through the cloud deck. Is what you see actually the ground, or is it just the top of another layer of clouds in the gray murk below?

You might want to circle for a moment to make sure. Remember this rule: any straight line you see, no matter how vague, indicates something man-made—in other words, something on the ground.

Okay, there it is, something straight, probably a road, although you can't be sure. Still, it indicates that you'll be able to get down without losing visual contact with the ground for any length of time. You briefly consider that technically what you're about to do is not legal because you won't be staying clear of the clouds, but forget that— right now, getting down safely is more important than worrying about the FARs.

If you're still thinking clearly and planning ahead, you'll now check your nav receiver for your exact position in relation to an airport, which you have to locate once you're below the clouds. You'll have to assume your descent will most likely be a shallow spiral in order to stay within the confines of that patch of thin clouds, and that you'll therefore be more or less at the same location below the clouds as you were above them.

These preparations are extremely important, because once below the clouds and relatively close to the ground, you might find that you've lost signals from the VOR you are currently using. Unless you know which way to fly and what landmarks to look for, you could end up running out of fuel while looking for the airport.

Once you know which direction and how far the airport is from your position, you're ready to descend. Regardless of how much or how little you are able to see of the ground, you'll have to be prepared to fly the descent by reference to the instruments alone because the turning radius of the aircraft is likely to be such that you'll be in and out of clouds all the way down.

So you throttle back, possibly apply carburetor heat just to play it safe, and trim the airplane to a comfortable 500 fpm rate of descent. You fly a shallow bank in order not to lose sight of your hole and try to maintain the rate of bank at a steady angle.

At first, this is all easy. It will take several minutes until you get to the tops of the underlying clouds. Then, quite suddenly, everything changes. Clouds stream by your windows at incredible speed, and even though the speed of your airplane hasn't changed, you have a feeling as if you were suddenly jet-propelled through the enveloping mess. Forget about looking for the ground. Right now, the only important thing to watch is the artificial horizon, the airspeed indicator, the vertical speed indicator, and occasionally maybe the altimeter.

It seems to take an incredibly long time before your peripheral vision senses the ground and you glance up and see a road, fields, a house. You're out of the clouds. You level off at 4,500 feet, which puts you some 2,500 above the terrain. You check the directional gyro against the magnetic compass to make sure that it's still pointing in the right direction, and you take up the heading you picked earlier to take you to the airport.

Okay . . . so you were lucky and made it all in one piece and you'll never do it again without first getting your Instrument ticket. But what if there hadn't been that convenient hole or the spot in the overcast? Or, you got spooked on instruments and lost control over the aircraft while circling? Let's analyze the various possibilities.

Possibility #1: The Solid Overcast

There is no hole. In this case, the worst thing you could do is to keep on flying and hoping until the fuel gauge needles hover on empty.

As long as you have fuel, you have control, but once the fuel is gone, you lose all options: you have to come down whether you want to or not, and you don't even have the luxury of picking a place to land once you're below the clouds.

In other words, don't procrastinate; make a decision while there is plenty of fuel to carry out your plan. And even then, be prepared to run one tank dry when there are still 10 or so gallons left in the other. It's silly to keep switching tanks until both are practically empty and neither can be counted on to take you that final distance to the airport.

So, with fuel getting low, but not yet critical, you pick an airport at which you want to land. You might want to pick one that is uncontrolled, since your descent through the clouds will be illegal, though it is highly unlikely that any tower controllers would see you break out of the bottom of an overcast, even right above the airport. Realizing that there is always the slight possibility that you could run into some IFR traffic while in the clouds, you now have to decide whether you want to talk to air traffic control or whether you prefer to simply bore a hole in the clouds and hope for the best.

Even without an instrument rating, the correct thing to do is contact the nearest Flight Service Station and tell them that you want to file IFR. They're not going to check your credentials—unless you don't sound as if you know what you're doing— they'll simply ask you to go ahead with your flight plan. But, you cannot file an IFR flight plan simply from VFR condition (above) to VFR condition (below). You have to have a destination. Thus, you will have to give your current position and altitude, a destination airport—regardless of whether that's where you want to land—your estimated arrival time based on the estimated ground speed of your airplane, and so on.

The FSS will ask you to stand by while they get ATC on the horn and file for you. After a while, sometimes 10 minutes or more, they'll get back to you with something like: "ATC clears Cessna one-two-three-four-Romeo to Middletown Airport direct. Descend to and maintain six thousand. Contact Kansas City Center on one thirty-four point nine, over." You are expected to read that clearance back to affirm that you have it correct, and if you're not ready, you probably missed about half of it. Have a piece of paper and a pencil ready to jot down such data as altitudes and frequencies. That will make the readback easier, and what's more important, it means you have it handy for later reference.

Once you have read back the clearance (correctly), you contact ATC on the center frequency and simply tell them: "Kansas City Center, Cessna one-two-three-four Romeo at one-one thousand, descending." They'll come back with something like: "Cessna three-four Romeo, radar contact. Report reaching 6,000." The clearance probably will also have included a specific transponder code, and ATC might ask you to ident in order to make sure that they are following the right aircraft.

Possibility #2: Still in the Clouds

The problem with such an IFR clearance is that the altitude to which you have been cleared might not actually be below the clouds. If that happens, contact ATC when reaching the assigned altitude and say, "Kansas City Center, Cessna three-four Romeo level at six, requesting four." They might give it to you, assuming that the requested altitude is at or above the minimum en route altitude (MEA) for the area.

If they won't clear you to the lower altitude, but you feel comfortable continuing in the soup, you can call them back and tell them that you're canceling IFR. They then assume you're in VFR conditions, even if you're not, and stop worrying about you. You can now drop down to VFR levels below the overcast, being reasonably sure you're not going to run into anyone because there is no IFR traffic below MEA.

The trouble with filing IFR is that ATC expects you to be proficient on instruments and capable of following controllers' directions. All of this doesn't sound too complicated sitting here reading it, but in the air—perhaps fighting turbulence or vertigo, worrying about remaining fuel, and wondering what ATC is going to tell you to do—it can be hairy.

The other option, short of simply coming down illegally without talking with anyone, is to call the nearest FSS and simply confess your predicament. Though in the end this might result in your suspension of privileges for three months or so, the FAA will at least do everything in its power to get you down safely and keep other traffic away from you.

Most probably, if there is a controlled airport in the area, the FAA will direct you to the airport and then give you a surveillance radar approach because it is the easiest to fly for someone with no instrument experience. It consists of a controller telling you which way to fly, which way to turn, and when to descend. Since he knows only where you are laterally, you must keep him informed as you pass through various altitudes. As long as you keep your head, this type of approach is a lead-pipe cinch.

One word about controlling the aircraft by reference solely to instruments— although it has been said and written thousands of times, here it is once again—our sense of balance is completely unreliable once visual reference to a fixed object such as the ground or horizon is lost. When the airplane banks for just a few moments, the inner ear, which controls our sense of balance, will stabilize, and tell us that we are flying straight and level. If we actually do level off, it will then try to tell us that we are banking in the opposite direction.

We must simply force ourselves to completely ignore the so-called seat-of-the-pants sensations and must place complete trust in the instruments. The primary instrument used for this purpose is the artificial horizon. Second, the airspeed indicator is used because a sudden reduction in speed will mean that we are climbing and might be approaching a stall; an increase in speed indicates a dive. The vertical speed indicator is also helpful, but its reactions tend to lag, causing us to overcontrol. The turn-and-bank indicator is useful in maintaining a steady angle of bank, although this can also be accomplished using the indications on the artificial horizon.

Whenever there is someone in the airplane who can look out the window and watch for traffic, it is a great idea to practice flying on instruments—straight and level, banking, climbing, and descending. At least then, if you ever have to do it, you know what to expect. While precision flying is of no particular importance when you are VFR, it becomes an absolute necessity the moment you find yourself in IFR conditions.

HEY! NO PROBLEM!

The flight from Wichita to Minneapolis-St. Paul was to take four business partners to see a photo processing operation similar to one they wanted to build. Since the pilot was one of their better customers and a newly minted private pilot, they suggested renting a 206 so he could fly them on the trip.

They left bright and early and headed northeast over low, patchy, puffy clouds, climbing to 7,500 feet, where the air was silky smooth and everyone was comfortable.

The pilot dialed one radio to the outbound radial from ICT and the other to an upcoming VOR in northern Kansas, then smartly snapped on the autopilot, poured a cup of coffee, and did his best imitation of the cool corporate pilot.

Everyone was enjoying the flight. They asked about flying. The pilot answered questions, demonstrated instruments and controls, and gave a mini-seminar on navigational aids. They were even brave enough to tell a few crash and burn jokes.

Glancing at the No. 2 VOR indicator, the pilot noticed it was picking up a strong signal, so he switched the frequency to No. 1 and began to search the charts for the next station.

"What kind of clouds are those?" the right front seat passenger asked, pointing through the windshield. There, about 40 miles dead ahead, were billowing white clouds growing out of a solid white base. The pilot glanced down. No holes, no thin spots, nothing but white. He looked behind. More of the same. Somehow, for the past hour he had been ignoring the outside world, and the thin scattered puffies they had left at home had all crowded together.

"Hey, no problem!" the pilot said confidently. "We'll just backtrack 'till we find a hole to go down through."

"But our appointment is at noon," one of the partners in the back shouted. "We've got to get there by noon!"

Hey! Wait a minute! This sounds like the beginning of all those accident stories we've been hearing.

"Can't you just go down through it like the airlines do?" the guy in the right seat asked, a look of utter trust on his face.

Well yeah, okay, sure! I've had, what? Three hours of hood time? Sure, I can just drop through this stuff, the pilot said to himself. I'll just pull the power back a little and we'll set up a 300- or 400-foot descent—straight ahead, no tricks.

The clouds began to envelop the Cessna, and he riveted his eyes to the instruments. He checked his watch. After 30 seconds, he stole a glance out the side window. Still nothing but foggy white. Back to the gauges—Whoop! slight correction there. Speed's okay, wings are level, down to 4,000 feet, only got another 1,500 or so before we hit green stuff. Glance again—Whoop! slight correction. Was that the ground? No. Whoop! slight correction.

The passengers were quiet, but confident. Suddenly, one of them said, "Wow! Look!" and pointed to the right. There was a 1,450-foot television tower at the three o'clock position, about 100 yards off the wingtip! The pilot looked at his Sectional. They were supposed to miss that obstacle by ten miles, and would have had he been keeping his heading, but in descending through the clouds, he had never consulted the directional gyro. They were on a heading of 013 instead of the intended 080 degrees.

The pilot quickly corrected the heading as if nothing were wrong. Maybe he had fooled his passengers; they didn't seem scared.

"I'm sure glad we got outta those clouds," one of them remarked, "cause every time you looked out the window, we banked about 30 degrees to the left and that little airplane on the instrument went way over!"

BETWEEN LAYERS

There are times when, in an effort to reach VFR conditions on top, the VFR pilot can get himself into a situation that could easily prove to be beyond his abilities.

It usually starts off simply, with low scattered clouds all over the place, and it seems perfectly logical to climb above them, even though there is a higher layer of broken or even overcast clouds above them. Or, at the time, there might not be such a high layer; it might only show up some miles farther along the way.

At first everything is fine. There are patches of blue between the clouds above, and much of the ground is often visible through the spaces between the lower clouds. The change is quite gradual and, at first, the pilot might not be aware of it. Both above and below, the open areas between the clouds are becoming smaller and smaller, until eventually there is no longer any friendly blue above or a reassuring visual contact below.

The airplane is now flying between layers, but the visibility is good and there are sure to be breaks farther on, so you might as well continue, right? Wrong! This is the time to pick up the mike and start calling people on the ground who can see the weather conditions ahead and to either side. This is the time to take stock of remaining fuel, to figure your range, and to immediately head in the direction for which reported conditions will guarantee getting down through the layer of clouds.

Even though the two layers between which you are flying at the moment might appear to be distinctly separate, the fact that they have turned from scattered or broken to solid is a fairly certain indication that things will continue to worsen, and odds are that somewhere ahead the two layers will start to merge into one thick layer, rather than two thin ones. When that happens, and it nearly always does, if you want to stay legally and safely VFR, you will have no choice but to turn around and try to get out by retracing your steps. Of course, there is no assurance that conditions behind you have stayed the way they were. They might have, but then again the clouds might have decided to build from the bottom up or the top down, leaving you with no alternative but to fly into instrument conditions.

CALL FOR HELP

There are no meaningful statistics about VFR pilots to whom getting caught between layers was fatal, because once such an accident has happened, investigators know only that weather was the cause, but usually have no way of reconstructing what took place earlier. And those pilots who manage to extricate themselves, legally or otherwise, usually would rather not talk about it.

And this brings us to one of the less obvious causes of many weather-related fatalities: the psychological block that stops the pilot from calling for help when he first finds out that he has got himself in a situation that might exceed his abilities. All of us hate to admit that we have done something dumb. In addition, as soon as we find ourselves in a situation that is no longer strictly VFR, we also tend to worry about the consequences that might result if we call some FAA facility and admit to being unable to continue VFR even though we're not instrument rated.

The fact is that all kinds of help is always as near as the microphone. All you have to do is pick it up and call somebody and tell them your predicament. Granted, they can't fly the airplane for you; that you have to do yourself. But what they can do is guide you to an area where conditions are more favorable and where you might be able to get back on the ground without endangering either yourself or others. And if there subsequently are any legal repercussions, they are certain to be considerably less serious than a bent airplane or worse.

All of this is easier to write down than to do under actual conditions. There is always a little voice in the back of your head that keeps saying, "maybe it'll get better soon," so you plow onward until the fuel gauge tells you that soon has arrived, and it's too late to expect anyone on the ground to do you much good. It can't be stressed too often: when things start to look bad, call for help. Don't wait!

MAINTAIN CONTROL

But when you do call for help, you shouldn't mentally relinquish the control of the airplane to the controller or flight service specialist. There are scores of recorded radio transmissions by VFR pilots in trouble where the pilot keeps repeating: "Tell me what to do, I don't know what to do . . . " That is ridiculous and a sure sign of panic on the part of the pilot.

You are the pilot in command, and no one on the ground can tell you what to do. They can suggest a heading. If the controller is a pilot and familiar with the type of airplane you are flying, he might suggest a change in altitude, airspeed, or such. But, all he can do is suggest. It is up to you to remain calm and in complete control. This, too, is easier said than done, but once you let panic take hold, you might just as well point the nose of the airplane at the ground and bore in because that's what might happen eventually anyway.

3
Visibility

THE TERM *VISIBILITY*, AS IT IS COMMONLY USED IN AVIATION, IS THE GREATEST horizontal distance at which an observer can identify prominent objects with the naked eye. In controlled airspace, the minimum visibility for legal VFR flight is three statute miles. In uncontrolled airspace it is one mile.

Judging visibility on the ground is usually accomplished by seeing a landmark for which the distance is known. Once in the air, on the other hand, judging visibility becomes strictly a subjective matter. The pilot looks out the window of his airplane and simply guesses how much visibility there is. Much of this is necessarily based on how far ahead he can see the ground, since in the air there is nothing to look at and judge, making it impossible to have a clear idea of how far one can see.

This presents no problem when it's relatively clear. The difficulty arises when you are flying in haze conditions. Relatively thick layers of haze tend to cover large portions of the country much of the time. What usually happens is that you can see the ground below without too much difficulty, but you don't have the faintest notion of how far you would be able to see another airplane if there was one at your altitude. In most instances, you are under the impression that the visibility laterally is less than it actually is, and when you finally do spot another airplane, you are surprised to find that you can see him quite clearly in all that soup even though, judging by his size, he is quite a distance away.

Flying in such hazy conditions, while technically VFR, more often than not requires that the pilot be able to control his airplane primarily by reference to his instruments because the horizon might be indistinct or totally invisible.

HARROWING HAZE

Let's take visibility haze conditions that are frequently present around various airports (FIG. 3-1). There are actually no clouds anywhere and the sun is clearly visible above, but lateral visibility is zilch—barely one mile.

Coping with haze can only come from experience. One low-time pilot flew a lot of eastbound trips at sunset that prepared him for a most unusual flight.

Less than 150 hours were in his logbook, but his business required flying eastbound while the sun was setting in the west. More often than not, a thick haze layer developed at the temperature inversion several thousand feet above the ground. When sunlight was diffused in the haze, the horizon disappeared momentarily in a gray muck. Then slowly but surely, streetlights of cities, towns, and farms would poke through for a better surface reference. Finally it would get dark at cruise altitude and the haze would "disappear."

It was an eerie sight that left the VFR pilot uncomfortable. Too often he would rely on an autopilot to keep the airplane on course, but with more flights he became more comfortable and would hand-fly the airplane referring to instruments—while also scanning for en route traffic conflicts.

Sometimes the inversion layer carried more than haze, with cumulus clouds extending above the layer in clear air. In this case, the pilot would stay lower than the

Fig. 3-1. *VFR pilot takes off into low-visibility haze conditions.*

inversion altitude, ensuring cloud avoidance when it got dark and the small buildups were not easily visible. He always looked for "veiled" ground lights or black holes that might indicate rain or some other weather. But on a trip one weekend, he would have to deal with extremely poor visibility, in haze, at a high altitude in an airplane with no autopilot.

The weekend was drawing to a close, and he planned to go home on Sunday afternoon. Unfortunately, an ugly squall line of thunderstorms lurked to the west, moving slowly east. Satellite photos showed the line stretching for several hundred miles directly on top of the route home.

Simple enough. He would wait until Monday morning when the front would be east of the route. Flying directly to work dictated a dawn departure. Weather was great—no wind, stars above—driving to the airport, but as the sun started to rise, it filled the skies with whiteness—a thick moisture-laden atmosphere that made it almost like a fog or one huge cloud.

Prior to departure, visibility was adequate with no cloud cover, and weather reports indicated conditions would remain unchanged through the morning. In calm air, climbing on course, visibility was about five miles.

He hoped to fly out of the haze at a higher altitude and kept climbing until he reached 8,500 feet. The haze appeared to extend another 1,000 to 2,000 feet higher, so he leveled at 8,500 with only a patch of ground directly beneath—no distinct horizon in sight.

Pilots occasionally refer to flying "in the milk bottle" when it is IFR in thick clouds and all you can see are wingtips and whiteness. The pilot decided he was in a bottle of "skim" milk, because the whiteness was just thin enough to see down.

This airplane had no autopilot, so unlike the airplane he was used to that could "fly itself" in poor visibility, the pilot had to keep it on course himself. But with no turbulence and perfect performance, it was easy to control.

Luckily it was a return trip to familiar territory and the home airport. Forward visibility was nil as landmarks passed under the wings. Normally, the airport would have been visible and its tetrahedron would be in sight just a few miles away. There was no hint of an airport, but the ADF was pointing to the airport's nondirectional radio beacon (NDB).

The pilot was getting skittish when the city north of the airport appeared. "The airport is supposed to be right there," he thought, but "there" was a dark gray mass that extended from the surface to above the airplane. Flying in whiteness and headed for grayness was not appealing, not to mention baffling.

A check with Unicom confirmed the suspicion that there was no rain and no wind, but why couldn't the airport be seen?

All of a sudden the plane passed through a thin cloud and emerged with the airport straight ahead in clear air—under the large shadow of a stationary cloud. Everything was visible under the cloud, and now everything outside the shadow was obscured where sunlight illuminated the haze. The approach and landing were uneventful, but he would never forget the "lost" airport.

A pilot unfamiliar with the area north of the airport might have missed it. Five miles either side would have been away from major landmarks; only the ADF would have pointed to the airport. Imagine what would have happened to a pilot with no ADF who was unfamiliar with the area.

Considering the possibility of dense haze on future flights in unknown areas, the pilot resolved to be more careful and respect it as a hindrance to safe operation of the airplane.

A FOILING FOG

Regardless of a pilot's ratings and a plane's state-of-the-art instrumentation, fog can render both useless. That curse simultaneously and separately hexed an IFR student and his instructor one Friday.

The instructor and his wife were in a Piper Arrow that taxied out in front of the IFR student in the Grumman American Cheetah. Both were headed northeast; the Arrow flying 200 miles farther than the Cheetah. The Arrow pilot had filed IFR; the Cheetah pilot, VFR. It was already dark when they took off into a crystal clear autumn night.

The Cheetah would fly direct to a VOR as the Arrow deviated to intercept a Victor airway. The Cheetah pilot monitored air traffic control (ATC), listening to his instructor's technique, but lost contact with the Arrow near the VOR. Both made it to their respective destinations without incident.

When the time came to return home Sunday, the Cheetah pilot had a bad case of "get-home-itis," and despite poor weather decided to try a flight, hoping the weather would improve after takeoff. Destination weather was poor, but VFR, so he decided to try it and turn back if necessary.

A thick but high overcast hung over the airport with scattered clouds underneath. Looking south, in the direction of his flight, the pilot could see large areas with no clouds under the overcast and good visibility, so he decided to leave.

Fifteen minutes after departure, he was ready to turn back. The scattered clouds he was flying over had gathered and were now broken, so he descended below them—and they promptly turned into a second overcast. Visibility was deteriorating, and a 180-degree turn seemed likely. But suddenly the visibility improved and he decided to continue, now planning to stop halfway and spend the night.

Stopping for the night was an exercise in itself; scud clouds surrounded the destination city, and rain with drizzle had started falling at the airport. Radar vectors from approach control included deviations to avoid clouds. Finally the Cheetah's tires touched down on wet pavement that, as it turned out, would not be dry anytime soon.

The weather quickly deteriorated into a steady rain with some heavy showers. Safe and dry in a motel room, he fell asleep to the sounds of rain on the roof, dreaming of sunshine and calm winds the next morning. Monday dawned gray, wet, and cold with some fog. Flying was hopeless, so he decided to check bus schedules and learned the only bus going his direction had just departed. If the weather did not improve, he decided to be on that bus on Tuesday, losing just a day and a half of work.

It got worse Monday afternoon as a thick fog settled over the area, disrupting all civil air travel. On the bus Tuesday, fog was so thick that visibility seemed to average about 100 yards. And it stayed that way Wednesday, Thursday, and Friday. His uncontrolled home airport was closed for several days.

The Cheetah pilot wondered if his instructor had returned in the Arrow before the poor weather settled in. Sure enough, his truck was at the main hangar while he probably enjoyed a "grounded" cup of coffee. He made it home under similar circumstances, but this time the Arrow pilot had eavesdropped on the Cheetah pilot.

While the Cheetah pilot was VFR and landing to sit out the weather, the Arrow pilot was IFR above the clouds and his student. While monitoring an approach frequency, the instructor heard his student getting vectored to the airport and considered giving his student a ride home, trying to reach the Cheetah on a Unicom frequency. But it was fruitless, as the airport's Unicom was 122.7 and the instructor was transmitting on the standard 122.8.

So the instructor continued, but the fog was settling in, forcing the home airport below the minimums of the NDB approach. He flew to a large en route airport with an instrument landing system (ILS) and shot the approach. By the time a friend arrived to take the instructor home, that airport was below minimums, too.

Both instructor and student were grounded by a cool and dense fog—the Arrow was 100 miles away and the Cheetah 200 miles away, both waiting for the weather to clear.

It was a rare instance where a pilot with all the ratings and an airplane equipped with state-of-the-art navigation gear could not get in the air. Fog ruled supreme.

Finally, the Arrow came home Saturday, six days late. It would be used Sunday to retrieve the Cheetah and it, too, got home . . . one week late.

SPECIAL VFR

There is one procedure that allows takeoffs or landings at controlled airports when conditions are below VFR minimums. It is called the Special VFR (S/VFR), and clearances are available at the pilot's request when visibility at the airport is at least one mile, but there is no minimum ceiling requirement, and all the pilot is expected to do is stay clear of the clouds (FIG. 3-2).

In practice, Special VFR works like this: airport conditions are IFR and the rotating beacon is indicating so. The sky might be partially obscured by haze, smoke, fog, or smog, with no ceiling. Visibility is restricted to one mile or a little better. There might be broken or solid overcast with bases below 1,000 feet and visibility below the cloud ranges anywhere from 1 mile to unlimited. The pilot who wants to depart on a VFR flight contacts ground control and requests a special VFR clearance.

The primary difference between an S/VFR clearance and an IFR clearance is that the S/VFR does not include a destination or specific altitude requirements. It will usually require the pilot to take up a specific heading immediately after takeoff and to remain on that heading, staying clear of the clouds, until he has reached VFR conditions above the haze or smog, or until he has left the control zone, which extends

Fig. 3-2. *Special VFR has no minimum-ceiling requirement.*

approximately five miles in all directions from the center of the airport. He is expected to inform the tower when he has either reached VFR conditions on top or when he has left the control zone—the latter usually being a more or less educated guess based on the time it will take the aircraft to cover five miles at an average ground speed.

If the pilot fails to request a special VFR clearance and simply tells the tower that he is ready for takeoff, the tower will inform him that the airport is IFR and ask, "What are your intentions?" The tower will not suggest that a special VFR clearance is available for the asking.

If an aircraft arrives in the vicinity of a controlled airport at which weather conditions are as just described, and if the pilot simply tells the tower before entering the control zone that it is his intention to land, he will also be told that the airport is IFR and will be asked his intentions. It is then up to the pilot to request a special VFR clearance.

When the clearance is given, it will usually call for flight to a downwind leg and a regular pattern, staying clear of the clouds. If there is a delay he might be asked to stay in VFR conditions outside the control zone or to hold above the airport at an altitude above the ceiling of the airport traffic area (3,000 feet above ground level—agl) until the clearance is available.

Delays are one of the primary inconveniences associated with S/VFR because all IFR traffic takes preference and because only one S/VFR operation may take place at one time in the control zone. The intervals between takeoff or approved clearances include the time it takes for each aircraft to leave the control zone or to fly from outside the zone to the airport and land.

Obviously, S/VFR is always associated with marginal weather conditions, and there are times when using it can take the pilot into some fairly tricky situations.

Haze

Let's take visibility haze conditions, which are frequently present at airports around Los Angeles, but also occur not infrequently in the Northeast and elsewhere. There are actually no clouds anywhere and the sun is clearly visible above, but lateral visibility is zilch, barely that one mile that makes S/VFR permissible. You are cleared for takeoff and requested to inform the tower when you have reached VFR conditions above the haze or when you have left the control zone. If this is at one of the L.A. airports, the haze or smog layer is likely to be only a few thousand feet thick, and you will probably break out on top before reaching the limit of the control zone.

Since there are no actual clouds, the standard warning phrase, "Remain clear of the clouds," is meaningless. But clouds or no, you will have absolutely no forward visibility. You might be able to see the ground below all right and the sun above, but laterally you might as well be in clouds for all the good looking out does you.

Aside from keeping the wings level by reference to your instruments, your primary danger during such a climbout is the tendency to stall the airplane. With no horizon or other outside reference available to help judge the angle of climb, it is only too easy to keep applying more and more back pressure. The answer is to watch the airspeed! Never mind trying to get out of the top of this muck in a hurry. If the airspeed starts to drop, get the nose down and let it build up again. An inadvertent stall—or worse, a stall-spin—this close to the ground more often than not is fatal. Airspeed is money in the bank, and that's what has to be watched above all!

In many other parts of the country the haze layer, especially on hot summer days, might actually be two or even three miles thick. In the average light aircraft there isn't a chance of getting on top of it. In this case, you report leaving the control zone and from then on you might find yourself surrounded by this awful soup for a long time, possibly the entire length of your flight. Straight down, you'll be able to see the ground, but at any kind of an angle, the ground quickly disappears into an indistinct blur. Lateral visibility in all directions will appear to be virtually zero, even though it is likely to be, in reality, several miles.

Since there is nothing to look at, the only way to obtain any idea of the actual lateral visibility is to look at the ground. If the airplane is at 10,000 feet agl and the ground can be seen reasonably clearly, then it is safe to assume that the lateral visibility is at least 10,000 feet, or 2 miles. It will be less later in the afternoon when the sun is at a low angle and you are flying toward it. At such times, the visibility toward the sun might be half or less of what it is away from the sun. One way or another, flying in such haze means flying by reference to the instruments.

One of the most unpleasant aspects of such haze conditions is the difficulty involved in finding the airport (FIG. 3-3). If there is a VOR or NDB right on the field, it's no serious problem even though you might not actually see the runway until you're

Fig. 3-3. *In smog or haze, you often can't see the runway until you are practically right on top of it.*

practically on top of it. If no convenient nav aid is available, you might have to stay high until you can see the airport below you. You'll then have to circle down, keeping the airport in sight all the time. If it's late afternoon and the sun is low, you should plan this descent in such a way that the airport is away from the sun. In other words, since the sun sets in the west, you will want to descend on the west side of the airport so that you have to look toward the east—away from the sun.

Low Overcast

Now let's look at another S/VFR situation. This one normally affects only departing aircraft. The visibility is such that you can see all the way to the next county, but there's a solid overcast hanging over the airport with cloud bases at, say 700 feet. Again, the airport is IFR, but with S/VFR having no ceiling minimums, an S/VFR clearance is legally available. In this case, you will level off right after liftoff and stay under the overcast until you are clear of the control zone. But what now?

Whether actually reported or not, if the overcast extends for a great distance, you might find that you will have to hedge-hop for mile after mile. And that's a lousy way to fly, considering all those chimneys and broadcast towers all over the place, not to mention the fact that it's illegal over populated areas. And if there are hills anywhere along your course, you might actually end up with no place left between the ground and the base of the clouds (FIG. 3-4).

In such a situation, the options tend to dwindle in a hurry. What you should have done was turn back as soon as you realized the apparent extent of the low overcast, but

Fig. 3-4. *If there are any hills ahead, you might end up with no room between the clouds and the ground.*

it's probably too late for that now. Instead, you keep following a road, trying to stay reasonably close to the direction in which you want to fly. But it won't be too long until, with all the nav aids being beyond reception distance at your level of flight, you no longer have a clear idea of where you are.

It's decision time. What next? There aren't really a great many choices left. You can land on a road, assuming this is one of the friendly states like California or Texas where they don't mind that sort of thing and will let you take off again when the weather improves. Other states, like New York for instance, are likely to insist that the airplane be dismantled and trucked to the nearest airport—an expensive and less than pleasant prospect.

But if landing on a road seems preferable to other options, then at least select one that is straight for a sufficient distance, with no telephone poles or power or telephone lines close to the side or crossing the road. Also, a little-traveled country road is preferable to a busy highway.

Barring such a precautionary landing, you can either continue, assuming there remains some space between the ground and the overcast, or you can shove in the throttle and climb into the clouds in the hope of reaching VFR conditions on top (FIG. 3-5). The latter is strictly against the rules, but once you have been stupid enough to get yourself into this kind of situation, altitude, regardless of the fact that it might be in the clouds, is still the safest way out, at least for a while.

As is true of virtually all of these marginal-weather conditions, you had better be able to control the aircraft by reference to instruments because at this point you are likely to have no idea of how long you will be in the clouds before breaking out on top—or not.

Some indication of the thickness of an overcast is the amount of light there was below it. If it was relatively dark, you must assume that the cloud deck might extend upward some 10,000 or more feet. Assuming that you'll be able to achieve an average

Fig. 3-5. *If it is getting light and there are breaks above, you might as well keep on climbing.*

rate of climb of some 400 fpm, you'll be in the soup for 25 minutes, which is a lot of instrument time for a nonrated pilot to enter in his logbook.

In situations like this, an autopilot or even a simple wing leveler is a great help. With that kind of mechanical assistance, all you have to do is trim the aircraft for a comfortable rate of climb and sit back and let it do the flying for you. Not only does this prevent you from giving erratic or incorrect control inputs resulting from the lack of sense of balance when deprived of outside visual reference, it also gives you time to study the charts and tune in whatever nav aids you believe to be within reception distance once you get to a reasonable altitude.

When you do finally start receiving signals from VORs, you will at least be able to determine with reasonable accuracy where you are. Once that has been accomplished, there are a number of actions you should take next, assuming that you are still in the clouds and it is sufficiently dark above to indicate that you may never reach VFR without having to climb to oxygen altitudes. If it is starting to lighten above and there are occasional breaks, it's probably best to simply keep on climbing and to start worrying about what to do next only after you have finally leveled off in the clear. But if it looks as if that is not going to be possible, then you have to decide what to do next.

The most sensible thing to do would be to contact an in-range FSS and file instruments. There is no need to tell them that you're already in the clouds. After all, they probably have no way of knowing what the conditions are at your position and altitude. While that would be the right and sensible thing to do, it must be assumed that having gotten yourself into this mess, you are not necessarily that sensible.

So, if you are determined to ride this thing out without having to deal with ATC, then you should take two actions without delay. One is to look on the chart and see where you are in relation to the Victor airways in the area. If there is any IFR traffic nearby, it is likely to be operating on the airways, and you would be a lot better off to stay away from the airway centerlines as much as possible. This doesn't mean that there might not be IFR traffic elsewhere; such traffic, operating by means of area navigation (RNAV) or Loran, might be found anywhere, but the chances of running into someone are at least considerably reduced.

The second action is to contact an FSS and ask for the conditions at all available reporting stations within a reasonable distance of your present position. After all, you want to get out of these clouds eventually, and the sooner you know where there is an airport with ample VFR conditions, the sooner you might be able to get back to somewhere where you can see where you are going.

In this kind of a situation, ample VFR conditions mean just that. If an airport is reporting 1,000 and three, that isn't good enough. Granted, it's VFR, but hoping to break out of the overcast just 1,000 feet above the ground is asking for trouble. Under such conditions, it would be necessary to fly a regular instrument approach, and obviously you neither know how to do that or have the appropriate approach charts in the aircraft.

As a rule of thumb, it would seem that 2,000 feet between the ground and the base of the overcast should be considered an absolute minimum. More is better. If there's a nearby airport with a 2,000-foot ceiling and one farther away with a 5,000-foot ceiling, it is probably better to head for the more distant one, even though that means you'll be in the clouds that much longer.

It goes without saying that if this is hilly country—or worse, mountains—the danger associated with dropping out of the clouds in hopes of being able to see the ground in plenty of time to control VFR flight toward an airport is considerably greater. Hills and mountaintops have a way of sticking up into the base of the clouds. Just because an airport located in some valley reports a 2,000- or 3,000-foot ceiling doesn't mean that the surrounding terrain might not be obscured.

If you have actually managed to find yourself in clouds above such terrain, you might find it necessary to plan the descent extremely carefully to be sure that you're coming down over lower country, and not into the side of a cliff. The best—and in some areas, the only—way to accomplish this is to pick out two VORs with a radial running from one to the other right along a valley or flat portion of ground with no obstacles in between. You then start the descent when established over one of the two VORs and fly toward the other one. As soon as that VOR is reached, you make a 180 and fly back along the same radial, or bearing, toward the first station. Throughout the maneuver, you keep looking down to be sure you see the first sign of the ground as soon as it appears through the base of the clouds.

This is pretty tricky stuff, and the best advice is to never get caught in clouds anywhere where there are hills or mountains.

ACCIDENT?

The pilot had taken off from Louisville at 10 P.M. one summer evening on a flight to Lansing, Michigan. He was a private pilot with just over 300 hours, alone, and flying a Skyhawk. The weather briefing he had obtained prior to takeoff indicated ample

VFR conditions along his entire route of flight, with the only reported weather being a line of thunderstorms moving toward Michigan from the northwest. There was more than adequate fuel aboard to make the trip nonstop even if, as the weather reports seemed to indicate, he would have to contend with some moderate headwinds.

His planned route of flight would take him over Muncie and Fort Wayne, Indiana, to the Litchfield VOR and from there to Lansing, a total distance of 285 nm. Even though he had not filed a flight plan, he contacted various FSSs along his route to report his position and to obtain information about any possible changes in the weather along his route and at his destination.

The flight proceeded without difficulty despite the high overcast, which obscured whatever light might have been available from the moon. The visibility proved to be excellent all along the way, and he congratulated himself on the precision of his navigation, which allowed him to hit every VOR right on the nose. Even his estimated time between nav aids turned out to be within a minute or so on each leg. At 1:48 A.M. he overflew the Litchfield VOR, and some seven or eight minutes later he contacted the Lansing Tower, reporting his position as 20 miles south of the airport.

The tower advised him to continue his approach, and he listened as they cleared a Learjet for takeoff. The pilot wondered if he would ever be able to cultivate that bored and tired sound that was the trademark of airline and professional pilots. Somehow you could always differentiate between the old timers and guys like himself by the way they sounded on the radio.

There were broken clouds below him, but he could clearly see the lights of the city through the wide open spaces between the clouds. He let down, and after a few minutes was able to see the rotating beacon of the airport on the far side of the city.

"Lansing Tower, Cessna Two-Five-Niner. How about a straight-in approach?"

"Cessna Two-Five-Niner, Roger. Make straight-in to Runway 32, wind 290 degrees at niner. Report two mile final."

He wondered how he was supposed to know when he was two miles out, but he acknowledged and decided he'd take a guess at it as he had always done. By now he was below the broken overcast and had the runway lights clearly in sight. He was just about to pick up the microphone to tell the tower that he estimated his position as being on a two-mile final, when they called him.

"Cessna Two-Five-Niner, Lansing. Do you read?"

Rats! The mike slipped out of his hand and dropped to the floor.

"Cessna Two-Five-Niner, Lansing. Do you read?"

He pulled the mike back up by its cord and pressed the button. "Ah . . . Two-Five-Niner."

"Roger, Two-Five-Niner, if you read now, the field is IFR, measured ceiling 900 broken, 3,000 overcast, visibility 10. Over."

"Two-Five-Niner." *So what . . . the airport is right there!*

"Two-Five-Niner, request your intentions. Over."

What does he mean by that? "Say again?"

"Roger, the field is IFR, request your intentions. Over"

What does he want? "I'm not reading you."

"Roger. The field is IFR with a measured ceiling 900 broken. Request your intentions. Over"

In the tower, the controller watched the landing lights of the approaching Cessna. Just as he was about to ask once more, the pilot's voice came over the speaker.

"I'll go on over."

"You'll be overflying the airport. Is that correct?"

"Right."

"Roger."

The controller picked up the direct line to the Flight Service Station and asked if there was a flight plan for an in-bound Cessna Three-Three-Two-Five-Niner. None was found.

A departing Westwind called Tower for his IFR clearance to Minneapolis. The controller gave the clearance, then cleared the jet for takeoff when it reached the end of the runway. He looked for a sign of the Cessna, but couldn't find any.

"Lansing Tower, Cessna Three-Three-Two-Five-Niner, do you read?"

"Two-Five-Niner, make right turn to the north. Advise you that the field is IFR and traffic departing Runway 27, over. Westwind Triple-Six Quebec, if you read, hold in position."

"Cessna Two-Five-Niner, Lansing, do you read?"

"I read you very well, Two-Five-Niner."

"Roger. The field is IFR. Turn to the north, fly to the north. Traffic departing Runway 27 going westbound. Report when you're clear of the control zone. Traffic is waiting to depart."

"Two-Five-Niner."

The controller waited a while, then called again. "Two-Five-Niner, I do not have you in sight now. How far are you?"

"Ah . . . fifteen miles."

"You say fifteen miles?"

"Affirmative."

"Roger, continue."

"Lansing, Westwind. What's it look like?"

"Westwind Triple-Six Quebec, cleared for takeoff and the Cessna says 15 miles out, but I'm not sure. He's supposed to be north."

"What altitude is he?"

"He appeared to be about 900. He's VFR. Cessna Two-Five-Niner, what is your altitude?"

"Two thousand five hundred."

"Roger, 2,500."

At this point the light on the direct line to the weather bureau lit up and the controller answered.

"Yeah, if you see any lightning, let me know. The radar indicates increasing activity all through the area here, but I don't see any lightning."

"No, I haven't seen any yet, either. I heard Center talking to Muskegon and they said they had a big line over that way."

"Yeah, there's some stuff . . . ah . . . 42,000 feet, over Grand Rapids direction, but I don't see it, don't see any lightning there."

"Cessna Two-Five-Niner, Lansing Tower."

"Lansing Tower?"

"Roger, Two-Five-Niner. Lansing weather is now measured ceiling 900 broken, 3,800 overcast. The field is IFR and . . . ah, request your intentions, over."

"I'm going over to Grand Rapids."

"Roger, you're proceeding to Grand Rapids, is that correct?"

"Affirmative."

Three-Three-Two-Five-Niner never landed at Grand Rapids. The wreckage and the fatally injured pilot were found the next morning in a field some six miles west-southwest of the Grand Rapids airport, having apparently impacted the ground in a near-vertical attitude.

The sequence of events just recounted is based on the NTSB transcript of an actual case. All the pertinent radio transmissions are exactly as they took place.

The reason for incorporating this unhappy occurrence here is to demonstrate how a controller, by performing his duty exactly by the book, can in fact become the cause of an accident.

After all, the Cessna was established on final approach and had the runway in sight, and there was no reason on earth for him not to continue and land, except that the airport suddenly turned technically IFR and thus, according to the rules, the pilot would either have had to request an instrument approach for which he was neither licensed or capable, or he could have requested a Special VFR approach.

Obviously, he was unaware of the S/VFR alternative, or the sudden and unexpected turn of events confused him so that he simply forgot.

Despite the fact that controllers, under normal conditions, are not authorized to suggest an S/VFR clearance to a pilot, this was clearly not a case of normal circumstances.

The controller could have even used a phrase such as: "Do you intend to request a Special VFR approach?" which would have satisfied the rules that he did not actually suggest such an action. Instead, by asking the pilot his intentions over and over, he most probably simply added to the pilot's confusion.

And then, to top everything off, when the pilot told him that he was going on to Grand Rapids, he did not inform him of the severe weather in that area, even though just minutes before, the weather bureau had mentioned buildups of 42,000 feet in the area.

An experienced VFR pilot, finding himself in this predicament, would either have simply pretended that he didn't hear the tower and would have landed or would have used the Special VFR available to him.

When a safe landing is clearly assured, it makes absolutely no sense to let oneself be diverted into a situation which, as in this case, can prove to be dangerous. Or fatal.

4
Wind

WIND OF A MILLION VARIETIES IS THE PRIMARY REASON WHY NO TWO landings are ever exactly alike. The best you can do is be prepared for the unexpected and minimize the chances for unpleasant surprises.

Winds will present problems to some aircraft, and to some pilots, both at altitude and on the ground. Winds of average velocity, say less than 20 knots, present no particular problem except that they influence ground speed and might, unless we pay close attention, move us off our desired course.

Stronger winds often produce uncomfortable turbulence and, especially in mountainous areas, severe up- and downdrafts. Winds, especially headwinds, must be figured in terms of percentages of the cruising speed of the airplane. In that respect, a slow airplane is much more seriously affected by headwinds than a fast one. An airplane with a true airspeed of 100 knots fighting a 25-knot headwind will move across the ground at 75 knots, only three-fourths of its no-wind speed, meaning that the distance between refueling points has to be reduced by 25 percent. On the other hand, a 200-knot airplane fighting the same wind will be losing only 12.5 percent of both its speed and range.

The basic rule during severe wind conditions is to pay closer than normal attention to navigation and be prepared to change plans when necessary.

TAXIING

Winds of average velocity have little if any effect on an aircraft when it is taxiing, but winds above 20 knots will make it necessary to keep your hands on the control yoke to prevent the rudder, ailerons, and when taxiing downwind, the elevator from being slammed against their stops. When taxiing into a strong front-quartering cross-wind, it is advisable to turn the aileron control as far as possible *into* the wind. This procedure will raise the upwind aileron, reducing lift being produced in that wing. If the crosswind is rear-quartering, turn the aileron control *away* from the wind.

Under extremely strong wind conditions, it might even be necessary to have someone walk along and hang onto the upwind wing, especially when the aircraft is a light, high-wing single, such as a Cessna 150 or 152, and this is even more important in gusty conditions. As a general rule, heavier aircraft and low-wing airplanes are generally easier to taxi in wind than are light, high-wing aircraft.

RUNUP

During the runup prior to takeoff, the airplane should always be faced directly into the wind so that sudden gusts don't have the opportunity to grab the control surfaces while the pilot is busy with his pretakeoff checks. On warm days, this also helps to prevent excessive heat from accumulating in the engine compartment while waiting for takeoff clearance.

TAKEOFF

Takeoff figures published in the owner's manual of all aircraft are based on certain assumed conditions, regardless of whether they are referring to the ground run or the distance required to clear a 50-foot obstacle. Unless otherwise specified, these conditions assume that the aircraft is at gross weight; that the runway is paved, smooth, and dry; that the takeoff is being made at sea level with an outside air temperature of 59°F (15°C); and that there is zero wind. They also usually state the recommended amount of flaps to be used.

It is unlikely that you will ever simultaneously experience all of these conditions during your flying career, so every flight will have to be an exception to the published figures.

Each variation in any of these assumptions will affect the takeoff distance. If the aircraft is below gross weight, the takeoff run will be reduced, although probably not by very much. If the runway surface is rough or wet or if the runway rises a few feet from your starting point to the other end, more distance will be required.

Similarly, if the temperature is above standard, a longer ground run will be needed to achieve liftoff speed. The same holds true when the airport is at an altitude higher than sea level.

By far the greatest variable is wind. Every knot of available headwind will increase the speed of the relative wind over the wings and, in turn, reduce the takeoff distance. This remains true as long as the wind is directly on the nose of the aircraft or, at least, not more than 30 degrees or so to either side. A strong crosswind, even though it might be blowing at less than a 90-degree angle, tends to have the opposite effect because the control surface deflections needed in order to keep the airplane going straight down the runway create a certain amount of drag, which increases the time and distance necessary for the airplane to accelerate to flying speed.

Airplanes have a published maximum crosswind component, beyond which it is not recommended that takeoffs or landings be attempted. This too, is based on the assumption that the aircraft is at gross weight and that the runway surface is smooth and dry. Although a superior flying technique might make it possible to successfully take off or land under somewhat higher crosswind conditions, less weight in the aircraft or slippery runway surfaces might call for a reduction in the maximum crosswind component.

Under such conditions, the width of the runway also should be taken into consideration. If it is 150 or 200 feet wide, the pilot of a single-engine aircraft might be able to start his takeoff run on the downwind side of the runway and angle his airplane several additional degrees into the wind. That would be possible by aligning it with the centerline. But this technique works only if the runway is smooth and dry. If it is slippery because it is wet, covered with even slight amounts of snow or ice, or bumpy in a way that would cause the wheels to intermittently lose firm contact with the runway, it might actually be better to start the takeoff run on the upwind edge of the runway, pointing the nose along that edge, and accepting a certain amount of drift across the width of the runway as the result of the crosswind.

In addition, under strong crosswind conditions, very little or no flaps should be used because, particularly in gusty conditions, they help create too much lift too soon. As the result of a gust, you might find yourself lifting off momentarily before the aircraft is fully ready to continue flight.

Try to hold all three wheels of the airplane firmly on the runway until the plane has reached slightly higher than normal liftoff speed. If the nosewheel is lifted too soon, the airplane might try to weathercock into the wind, making control even more difficult.

As soon as the airplane is airborne, assuming there are no major upwind obstacles, turn the nose into the wind. Do not attempt a downwind turn until you have achieved ample flying speed and altitude.

Even though, once airborne, the aircraft theoretically moves with relation to the block of air within which it is located, and not with relation to the ground, gravity does exert a degree of influence on the movement of the airplane. Although the airplane theoretically continues to fly at a steady airspeed regardless of whether it is turning upwind or downwind, it does take a moment for the airspeed in the new direction to stabilize.

For instance, if you were climbing out at 100 knots with a 25-knot, 90-degree crosswind, when you make a 90-degree turn into the wind, the airspeed will momentarily increase—not all the way to 125 knots, but to a speed above 100 knots. As a result, the airplane will want to climb more steeply. Conversely, if you make a 90-degree turn downwind, you will momentarily lose some portion of that 25 knots, and the airplane will tend to sink, with that tendency being further aggravated by the bank angle of the wings. Thus, you should not attempt such a downwind turn after liftoff until you are high enough to accept a degree of altitude loss without endangering yourself or the aircraft.

CLIMBOUT

A similar effect can be experienced during the early phases of the climbout if the wind is disturbed by ground obstacles such as hangars, trees, hills, etc. It then tends to burble with constant and unpredictable variations in direction and velocity, more often than not having a detrimental effect on the airspeed and, in turn, the ability of the airplane to gain or maintain altitude.

During climbout, you gradually move from the area where winds and the associated turbulence are directly affected by ground-based obstacles into the realm where the winds are usually stronger, but where the air is more often smooth. Whether you prefer to climb steeply at, say, the best rate of climb, or more gradually at a cruise-climb setting is largely a matter of personal preference, although it might still be affected by certain other factors.

Since visibility over the nose of an aircraft is less than satisfactory when the aircraft is in a nose-high attitude, you might prefer to keep the nose somewhat lower, especially if you are climbing in an area where there is traffic. Conversely, on hot days when low-level thermals can cause extremely uncomfortable turbulence within several thousand feet of the terrain, you might want to get up as fast as possible and might, therefore, prefer to use a steeper angle of climb.

Although psychologically you might feel that cruise climbing is the more economical method of getting to your cruising altitude—because while climbing, you are also covering a lot more ground—this is actually a misconception. The difference in the overall time en route as well as the amount of fuel consumed between a steep and a shallow climb is so minimal as to be meaningless in most aircraft. Thus, the angle of climb is a matter of pilot preference, rather than economics or time.

CRUISE

The cruise portion of a flight is normally the longest in terms of time, and the portion during which most of the fuel is being used. It is, therefore, also the portion during which you want to be as comfortable as possible and take the greatest advantage of favorable winds or try to minimize the effects of unfavorable winds.

As a general rule, weather moves across the United States in a semicircle from the northern Pacific southeastward toward the Gulf of Mexico, and then turns northeastward toward New England before disappearing over the Atlantic Ocean. This means that the prevailing winds, at altitude, tend to be northwesterly in the western portions of the country, westerly in the central and south-central states, and southwesterly in the east.

This flow, with occasional variations, can be expected to exist at altitudes of 18,000 feet and above. Most of the time the velocity of these winds is strongest between 35,000 and 45,000 feet, decreasing both above and below (which is the primary reason why bizjet manufacturers have spent millions to obtain certification to altitudes above 50,000 feet).

For all practical purposes at the altitudes at which most of us like to fly, you can expect to fight headwinds when you're headed west, and tailwinds when going east. Thus it frequently makes sense to plan on higher cruising altitudes for easterly flight, but lower levels when going the other way. But, as all of us manage to figure out only too soon, there are never enough tailwinds to make up for the headwinds. One reason is that even if you fly identical distances in opposite directions—one with a tailwind and the other with an identical headwind—the headwind always wins out.

Figure it this way: You're flying a distance of 300 nm in an airplane cruising at 150 knots. With a 20-knot tailwind, you will cover that distance in 1³/₄ hours. But when turning around and flying back with a 20-knot headwind, it'll take 2 hours and 18 minutes. This means that you will be exposed to the detrimental effect of the headwind for 33 minutes longer than the advantageous effect of the tailwind.

In practice, especially with the high cost of today's fuel, this translates into certain sensible operating practices. When you are able to take advantage of a tailwind, the sensible thing to do is to slow down to a speed that approximates the ground speed you could have expected in nonwind conditions, thus giving yourself the opportunity to take advantage of the free push for a longer period of time. When fighting a headwind, on the other hand, it is prudent to increase the airspeed despite the attendant increase in fuel flow because this action will decrease the time during which you are being held back by the flow of air.

Wind components also determine, to some extent, the altitudes you should select for cruise. A light headwind at altitude might be preferable to no wind or even a light tailwind close to the ground because you burn less fuel with the lean mixtures at higher levels of flight, and at the same time achieve a meaningful increase in true airspeed, probably sufficient to negate the wind differential. But if the wind high up is considerable, say 15 knots or more, you would probably fly faster and cheaper—although not necessarily more comfortably—at a low altitude, despite the higher fuel consumption at the necessarily richer mixtures.

Aircraft equipped with turbochargers and supplementary oxygen can frequently, especially on eastbound flights, take advantage of some pretty sensible winds. On one flight from Portland, Oregon, to the East Coast in a Turbo Centurion, I remember moving across the ground at a speed in excess of 450 knots. The airplane has a normal TAS of somewhere between 155 and 160 knots. I was flying at 23,000 feet, where the tailwind component apparently added up close to 300 knots. The flight was as smooth as silk, and it was amusing to have controllers on the ground asking, "What kind of an airplane is that you're flying?'' But these days, with all airspace above 18,000 feet being under positive control, such flying does require an instrument ticket and appropriate instrumentation in the airplane.

Since winds aloft forecasts are notoriously inaccurate, keeping track of the actual wind and its effect on ground speed is especially important during extended cross-country flights in slower aircraft with relatively limited range.

To illustrate, a 100-knot airplane with a no-reserve range of four hours can theoretically cover 400 nm. By sticking to a prudent 45-minute reserve, this range is reduced to 325 nm. If you now add a wind factor of, say, 25 knots on the nose, the remaining ground speed is 75 knots, which, with $3^{1}/_{4}$ hours of flying time, results in a range of only 244 nm. By contrast, a 130-knot airplane with sufficient fuel for six hours (or $5^{1}/_{4}$ with a 45-minute reserve) can cover 682.5 nm in no-wind conditions and 551.25 nm with a 25-knot headwind.

In the first instance, the range reduction amounts to 25 percent. In the second example, the headwind cuts the range by somewhat less than 20 percent. This shows that, in terms of percentages, the ground speed, and in turn, the range of an aircraft, is affected to an increasingly lesser degree the higher the available airspeed.

The tendency of many pilots to preplan refueling stops and then to be loath to change those plans is a bad one. You must always remain sufficiently flexible to change your mind when wind conditions are other than had been expected or forecast.

DESCENT, APPROACH, AND LANDING

The final phase of any flight is always thought of as the one requiring the greatest concentration, and here is where winds can play unpleasant tricks. In order to be prepared, to know what to expect once you embark on the final stages of the approach, it is helpful to know in advance the surface wind conditions at the airport. If it is a controlled airport, this information will be provided by either the tower, once you announce your intention to land, or by monitoring the Automated Terminal Information Service frequency. If it's an uncontrolled airport, the Unicom operator might do the same thing, but remember that his, most probably, is simply a guess or an approximation. Where no Unicom service is provided, the best you can do is call the nearest FSS and use the information provided by them, remembering that, depending on the distance of the FSS from the airport, the information might not be terribly accurate.

What it's all about is the effect for which shifting or gusting winds have on the pattern and the final approach. Assume that Runway 36 is the active runway and that the wind is blowing from the northwest at 20 knots. Depending on the speed of the aircraft and the exact direction of the wind, you might find that you have to hold a 20-degree correction to the right while flying the downwind leg. This means that the change of direction from downwind to final approach is not the usual 180 degrees, but rather 220 degrees, because on final it will require the same 20-degree correction, except this time it is to the left.

Along the way the base leg is likely to give you trouble. If you have flown the downwind leg at the usual distance from the runway, the wind might cause you to drift past the final approach path, in which case you might have to turn even farther to get lined up with the runway. In this kind of a situation, it is often advisable to fly the downwind leg somewhat farther from the runway than usual, and you might find that you want to skip the base leg altogether and substitute a continuous, relatively shallow turn.

Keeping the turns shallow—even if that means that you end up having to go around and try again—is important because if you see that you are about to drift past the final approach path, you are likely to want to steepen the bank. That impulse, and the usually associated impulse to use bottom rudder, should be resisted because there is always the ever-present danger of getting into a stall-spin, recovery from which would be impossible at this altitude.

Also remember that frequently there is a difference in wind velocity at different distances from the ground (FIG. 4-1). If the wind velocity increases rapidly with altitude, as is frequently the case, the upper wing of an aircraft in a steep bank might actually be surrounded by air that is moving faster than the air affecting the lower wing. This would increase the lift produced by that upper wing and cause the bank to steepen even more.

The best practice during gusty crosswind conditions is to fly a wider and longer-than-usual pattern in order to give sufficient time to make whatever adjustments are necessary without haste (FIG. 4-2). Under these circumstances, a clearance from the tower for making a short approach should always be rejected.

Fig. 4-1. *Turbulence tends to be worse close to the ground than higher up.*

Fig. 4-2. *During every approach, when you get close to the surface you must always be prepared to make instant corrections in the event of sudden wind shear.*

Although it is generally preferable to fly a complete pattern, few of us would be inclined to reject a straight-in approach when it is given by the tower. The advantage is that you don't have to bother with those tricky turns into or away from the wind. The disadvantage is that you might set up what appears to be a just-right rate of descent to touch down on the numbers only to find that, as the result of changes in wind velocity, you suddenly sink at a faster rate than expected and are in danger of undershooting, but the exact opposite also can occur. During such a long straight-in approach, or during any final approach, you must always be prepared to make instant corrections.

Again, less than usual flap settings, or no flaps at all will simplify the task of landing in gusty or crosswind conditions. Avoid full flaps if at all possible because a sudden gust hitting them could make control of the airplane difficult.

Also, during the final phase of approach, you should never be tempted to lower the nose. Hold it up, and if excessive sink is being experienced, add a bit of power. Lowering the nose could easily result in a touchdown nosewheel-first. At best, the airplane will start to porpoise or wheelbarrow, and the pilot will frantically try to use the controls to overcome the situation. At the same time, there is virtually no control over the direction in which the airplane is moving because all three wheels must be firmly in contact with the runway in order to provide directional control. In addition, nosewheel structures being less sturdy than those of the main gear, a hard nose-low touchdown could easily break the gear and, in turn, damage the prop, making the whole arrival a rather expensive affair.

CROSSWIND TECHNIQUES

For those VFR pilots trained in windy country, learning to make successful landings when the wind is other than straight down the runway is tantamount to being licensed. To those used to gentle breezes right on the nose, a crosswind touchdown can be traumatic.

By far the most desirable technique is to set up your approach with the upwind wing slightly low, so as to minimize extra lift on that wing from sudden gusts, then to keep the nose of the aircraft lined up with the runway solely by using the rudder. Although this technique effectively puts the airplane into a slip, it tends to keep the pilot from trying to steer the airplane with aileron control.

WIND SHEAR

Wind shear is more a product of severe weather than of wind. An explanation of wind shear and downbursts is covered in chapter 8.

JUST DROPPING IN

It was an early spring day, and March was living up to its legend, with south winds of 25 knots, gusting to 30. Winds aloft for the flight from Wichita to Dallas were discouraging: 35 knots at 5,000 feet right on the nose, progressing to 45 a few thousand feet higher. The pilot decided reluctantly to cut his losses by bumping along at 3,500 feet in the Cessna 182.

After spending an hour fueling and filing, the pilot realized that he would not be able to make the 300 nm flight before sunset, so after taking off he refiled to Oklahoma City, some 130 nm away, where he knew he could spend the night with friends.

Nearly two hours later, he tuned in the Wiley Post Airport ADIS and found that surface winds were 210 degrees at 30 knots, gusting to 40. He called the tower and was told he would be landing on 19 Right.

When he could finally distinguish the runway in the late afternoon haze, he found that it was short and narrow, one which made him a bit uneasy in these conditions. Picking up the microphone, he requested a change to the longer 19L, but was denied because of other traffic that was inbound. He set up a straight-in approach and fixed his gaze on the runway, concentrating on staying on the correct descent path and heading, which was difficult in the gusty conditions.

At last he was nearing the approach end of the narrow runway, and began to ease power off, being careful to keep enough speed and power to be able to recover should anything go wrong.

Still 100 feet off the ground, the airplane suddenly plunged toward the runway, accompanied by the unmistakable whooshing sound of a stall. All that could be seen through the windshield was grass and asphalt. The pilot shoved the throttle forward to its stop, resisting the impulse to pull back on the yoke until he thought hitting the ground was inevitable.

The airplane struck the runway squarely on all three wheels, bouncing some 30 feet back into the gusty air, giving the pilot another chance to make a somewhat controlled landing. The second touchdown was more successful, and the 182 rolled to a stop.

Collecting his composure and looking about to see if there were any witnesses or anyone else he could blame, he saw the cause of his sudden plunge: about 100 feet to the right (and upwind) of the runway were some small trees. It was clear that the wind blowing across this obstacle created a flow of less velocity and of unstable quality. It was like a man-made wind shear.

The pilot made a mental note to, in the future, not give all his attention to only the runway, but to check out the surrounding terrain and features as well.

5
Turbulence

MOST TURBULENCE ENCOUNTERED IS SIMPLY AN UNCOMFORTABLE nuisance. It can be caused by a variety of conditions: gusting winds, wind blowing over mountains or other ground obstructions, rising warm air, or the atmospheric activity in the vicinity of thunderstorms.

CAUSE AND EFFECT

Though officially classified as light, moderate, severe, and extreme, judging the severity of turbulence depends on the pilot's susceptibility to the resulting discomfort, and on the size, type, weight, and speed of the airplane involved. Airplanes are built to be able to withstand huge amounts of turbulence, and the danger associated with severe turbulence is usually not one of structural damage to the airplane, but rather the chance of the pilot losing control. In an effort to regain control, a pilot might inadvertently cause stresses that exceed the limits of the aircraft structure.

As a general rule, it is advisable to reduce the speed of the aircraft somewhat and not to constantly try and correct for up- or downdrafts. Let the airplane bounce around and try to limit control inputs to those necessary to stay on course and maintain adequate obstruction-clearance altitude.

Most of the time, conditions near the ground tend to be more turbulent than at higher altitudes, although this is not always the case. The worst turbulence is that associated with thunderstorms—which no aircraft should be flown into intentionally.

Turbulence has held general aviation back more than gravity, but, like inflation and taxes, it is always with us. It is virtually impossible to ever expect to complete a flight from beginning to end without getting involved in some degree of turbulence. Although the average turbulence, while uncomfortable, does not represent any danger, it is important to know how to deal with it when it suddenly hits us full force.

It comes in all shapes and sizes, from a little friendly choppiness to incredibly hard bumps to a continuing series of up- and downdrafts. It tends to be most frequent and intense near the ground, although there is clear-air turbulence (CAT) reported occasionally at altitudes 10 miles above the earth.

Although we know that turbulence is the result of movement of the air, either in the form of wind, suction provided by thunderstorms, or thermal activity, which develops when the sun heats the ground, the study of turbulence, especially the clear-air variety, has been an inexact science.

We can't see turbulence unless it is associated with something visual like clouds, smoke, or blowing sand and dust. We can form educated guesses about the areas in which turbulence will be strong when known winds blow across mountains or other ground-based obstructions. We have read about and might have experienced the wake turbulence produced by large aircraft, and have been warned about the serious dangers associated with the wake turbulence created by slow-flying heavy jets during takeoff or landing. But we have virtually no way of knowing or avoiding clear-air turbulence.

Clear-air turbulence is thought to be the result of waves of moving masses of air coming up against denser air and breaking, much like ocean waves when they approach the shore. No one seems to know for sure, and in the final analysis, knowing what causes it isn't of much help in avoiding it. If you get hit by it, all you can do is slow the airplane down to maneuvering speed and ride it out.

Since we're relatively helpless to avoid CAT, and since most of it is experienced at higher altitudes, we'll concentrate on the kind of turbulence that most affects general aviation aircraft—that which is produced by wind or temperature variations and is found at altitudes up to 15,000 feet or so.

MOUNTAINS

Much wind-related turbulence is concentrated in areas of hilly or mountainous country. Here the surface winds are pushed upward as they hit the hills or mountains, and in turn push the air above farther upward. Once past the peak, the air tumbles down, much like a breaking ocean wave, pulling the air above it down in turn. In consequence, even though you might actually be cruising several thousand feet above the highest portion of the terrain, you are still likely to be subject to ground-induced turbulence.

Among and near the higher mountains you are faced with unique wind and turbulence problems (FIG. 5-1). Winds blowing through passes and valleys are subjected to a venturi effect that can, at times, increase their velocity as much as 100 percent.

Fig. 5-1. *Flying over mountains on a hot summer afternoon can prove to be most uncomfortable.*

Winds blowing across ridges will cause sustained and often smooth updrafts, which can push an airplane upward at 1,000 or more feet per minute. But as soon as they pass the top of the ridge, they'll spill down just as steeply, often resulting in downdrafts that might exceed the climb capability of the aircraft.

In this type of country, trying to escape turbulence, whether resulting from heat or wind, is a hopeless endeavor unless you're flying a jet, or at least a turbocharged aircraft equipped with oxygen.

One unique and potentially dangerous phenomenon associated with mountains is the so-called mountain wave. Soaring pilots seek out mountain waves because of the tremendous altitudes that can be reached by riding them. What happens is that fast-moving air hits the side of a mountain and flows upward in continuous waves, which might extend for great distances beyond the actual mountains. The upper portions of such mountain waves are generally smooth and might result in a continuous updraft, which might require a throttle reduction if you want to stay out of oxygen altitudes.

Below the mountain wave on the lee side of the mountain, something quite violent develops. Here is an area of turbulence, referred to as the *rotor*, where the fast-moving wave air conflicts with the normally undisturbed air at lower levels, causing rolling and tumbling air masses that, in extreme cases, might actually be violent enough to tear a light aircraft apart. The danger signs are lenticular clouds. These distinctively shaped clouds—which look like lenses, hence the name—tend to sit right on top of the worst areas of turbulence. They appear deceivingly calm, but the prudent pilot should carefully avoid flying under them.

Although mountain waves of serious proportions are usually only found over the higher ranges, such as the Sierra Nevada or the Rockies west of Colorado Springs, the wave can, to a minor degree, be experienced in the vicinity of all kinds of smaller mountains and even hills.

WAKE TURBULENCE

There has been much talk about wake turbulence, and it constitutes a potential danger to general aviation aircraft, so let's look at the best way to avoid it.

Wake turbulence is a condition that results when large, heavy aircraft, predominantly jets, are flying in the slow takeoff or approach/landing configuration (FIG. 5-2). The turbulence consists of two horizontal tornadoes generated by the wingtips of the aircraft, which rotate in opposite directions toward one another. In still air, they might remain behind the aircraft and slightly below its flight path for several minutes.

Wake turbulence must not be confused with jet blast. Wake turbulence is generated only at the point where there is maximum lift on the wings, meaning that there is no wake turbulence as long as the wheels of the aircraft remain in contact with the runway, or as soon as the wheels touch down during a landing.

With this in mind, a light aircraft operating behind a heavy jet should adjust its flight path to stay out of the areas in which these invisible tornadoes can expect to be found.

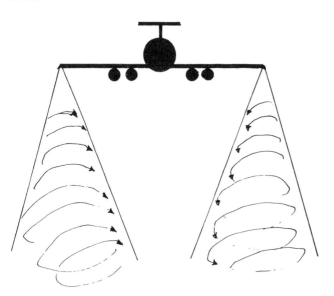

Fig. 5-2. *Wake turbulence is produced by slow-flying heavy jets.*

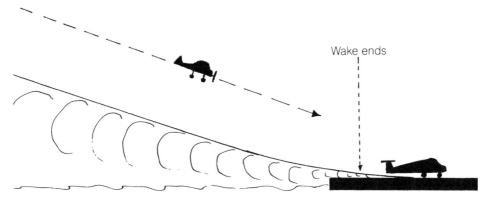

Fig. 5-3. *When landing, stay above the flight path of the jet.*

Landing after a Heavy Jet

When cleared to land behind a jet, the tower usually will include a warning, such as, "Caution; wake turbulence from landing 747," as part of the clearance.

Stay above the flight path of the landing jet (FIG. 5-3). Note the point on the airport at which its wheels touch down. Then plan your own landing in such a way that you touch down beyond the point at which the jet's wheels touched down. This might be a fair distance down the runway, but there should be ample room for you to bring your aircraft to a stop, considering that the jet, too, must have sufficient runway left after its touchdown to slow to a speed that permits it to turn off the runway.

If you feel funny about staying fairly high above half the runway, you might want to tell the tower that you plan to land long, beyond the jet's touchdown point.

If there is a crosswind, the wake turbulence will move downwind of the actual approach and landing path. In that case, staying slightly upwind of the flight path of the jet will add a degree of extra safety.

Takeoff after a Heavy Jet

When giving takeoff clearance behind a departing jet, the tower usually will include a similar warning in the clearance. In this case, the routine would call for you to lift off before reaching the point at which the jet's wheels leave the runway (FIG. 5-4). Then climb steeply to stay above the jet's departure path and turn to one side or the other, away from that path as soon as possible. If there is a crosswind, always turn into the wind to put as much distance as possible between yourself and the departing jet's wake turbulence.

All aircraft, no matter their size, create a certain amount of wake turbulence, but it's only serious in the case of larger aircraft. Once these aircraft have cleaned up all the high-lift devices they employ during landing and takeoff, the amount of wake tur-

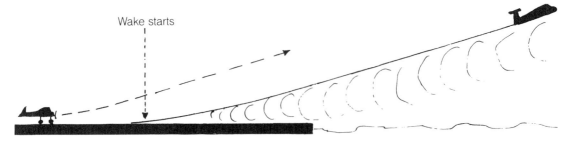

Fig. 5-4. *When taking off, lift off before the point where the jet's wheels left the runway.*

bulence is greatly reduced and no longer considered dangerous. But if you stray into a portion of air through which a jet flew a few moments earlier, you might still experience a sudden and violent bump. Therefore, when operating in the vicinity of airports with heavy jet traffic, it is always a good precaution to keep track of where the jets are and where they are going. Give them a wide berth.

6
Flying the Mountains

WHILE THERE IS NOTHING MARGINAL ABOUT MOUNTAIN COUNTRY FOR pilots who must fly in it all the time, for eastern and midwestern pilots, who do most of their flying in parts of the country where altitudes below 5,000 feet will clear all obstacles, a first flight across the Rockies is quite an eye-opener. There is something both scary and exciting about looking at charts that are printed mostly in varying shades of brown. One's mind's eye can't help but visualize towering peaks, steep cliffs, and deep valleys, which shrink the size of the airplane by comparison.

Questions come to mind that have never been important as long as one stayed in the flatlands. Will the service and absolute ceiling of the airplane clear the highest point along the planned route? How long will it take to get to those altitudes, and how much runway will be needed to get safely off the ground when the airport is at 6,000 or 7,000 feet msl? What about the weather? Is it likely to be much like that in the rest of the country, or is it, too, different? And the winds—what about those up- and downdrafts that people keep talking and writing about?

These days, with more and more business and industry concentrated in the West, the need to negotiate this high-altitude third of the country is becoming more and more important to an increasing number of pilots. That many attempt these flights while being inadequately prepared is borne out with depressing frequency by reports of light aircraft—many of them high-performance singles and light twins—that are reported missing and often not found for months.

Still, mountain flying can be perfectly safe if adequate precautions are taken and if the pilot bothers to become acquainted in advance with a few special techniques.

PREPLANNING

For the purposes of this chapter, let's plan a flight from Omaha to San Diego in a Cessna Skyhawk. This area covers much rough country, and the aircraft—although marginal for mountain flying—continues to be the most popular and numerous in the general aviation fleet.

First, we need charts with the most detailed topographical information—in other words, Sectionals. WACs might be acceptable for the more experienced, but only pilots who know the Rockies like the back of their hands should attempt such flights equipped with the low-altitude radio facility charts—and even for them, that is not the smartest thing to do.

To permit intelligent planning of the route to be flown, first analyze the performance parameters of the aircraft. Our Skyhawk, vintage 1975, has a maximum no-reserve range of 773 nm at 55 percent power. At this power setting, it produces a true airspeed (TAS) of 103 kts. Prudence dictates making a fuel stop with at least a one-hour reserve left in the tanks. Furthermore, we know from experience that there will be headwinds at altitude on any westbound flight. Taking these two factors into consideration, the actual range of the aircraft has now been reduced to 537 nm.

Another performance figure of importance is the service ceiling. For the Skyhawk, this figure is 13,100 feet. Since some of the higher peaks along the way reach above 14,000 feet, we simply can't plan to fly a straight line.

The shortest route would seem to be Omaha—Denver—Las Vegas—San Diego, so let's take a closer look and see what that entails. Although the terrain between Omaha and Denver rises from 1,000 feet to 5,000 feet msl, this leg involves no problems. The distance is 420 nm, which is easily within the range of the aircraft. But just beyond Denver, we suddenly face that 14,000-foot wall of rock, and from then on the flight is anything but routine.

If you arrive in Denver in the early afternoon, there is plenty of daylight left, especially in the summer. To add a respectable number of miles to the day's travel is tempting. However, the prudent pilot will decide otherwise. During the afternoons and early evenings, thunderstorms often build in the Rockies with impressive rapidity and can obscure mountaintops. Also, heat-generated turbulence is at its nerve-wracking worst. So the intelligent decision would be to stay in Denver, have a swim and a leisurely dinner, go to bed early, and be ready to take off the next morning as soon after dawn as possible.

There are good reasons for starting early. The mountains are the most beautiful during the early morning and late afternoon. The winds are likely to be relatively calm and last evening's thunderstorms will have dissipated, leaving just a few harmless puffs of cloud here and there.

The distance from Denver to Las Vegas is 542 nm, which is more than should sensibly be attempted without refueling, especially considering that the flight involves long stretches of hostile real estate where airports are few and the distances between them long. The intelligent thing to do is to plan to refuel at Grand Junction and then go on to Las Vegas.

It's 194 nm from Denver to Grand Junction as the crow is said to fly. Except we're not crows. The way we'll have to plan our route is considerably longer. We cannot sensibly expect our airplane to climb to an altitude that would take us safely across the 14,000-foot mountains west of Denver, not to mention that it would require oxygen, which we don't have on board.

The northerly and somewhat shorter detour involves Victor 8, leaving Denver in a northwesterly direction. This route necessitates an immediate climb to 12,000 feet in order to get over even the lowest pass, which means that it might take a few S-turns or even 360s to get up there before getting too close to the mountains. This is important because, with the probability of westerly winds, we're likely to encounter downdrafts close to the eastern slopes.

Visually, the easiest landmarks to follow are a railroad, highway, and mountain stream, all heading straight west toward Corona Pass. But watch out! The railroad disappears into the 7-mile-long Moffat Tunnel. Just northwest of the mouth of that tunnel is Corona Pass. Once through, we again pick up the same railroad and a highway—a different one—which lead us northwestward toward Kremmling and the Colorado River. The river flows from there to Grand Junction and can be followed easily. Once through that pass, we'll also be able to receive the Kremmling VOR.

However, for much of the time the Kremmling area is covered by clouds, the bases of which frequently obscure higher terrain. Therefore, unless the weather at Kremmling is reported to by strictly VFR, it might be better to plan for the southern and somewhat longer route.

This second route involves leaving Denver southwesterly on Victor 89 and then picking up Victor 95 at the Lake George Intersection. Following this route, we have all kinds of time to get up to altitude, but eventually here, too, a 14,000-foot mountain ridge lies across our path. At that point Victor 95 ceases to be of value to us, which is just as well because we most probably have lost reception from any of the referencing VORs. A railroad and road combination intersects V-95 at Buena Vista, which we can follow south.

At Poncha Springs the road, accompanied for a time by a railroad and the Arkansas River, heads west toward and eventually through Monarch Pass. By following it we can stay at a reasonable altitude and, once through the pass, the Gunnison VOR will come in. We can then use it or the Tomichi Creek to Gunnison and the Blue Mesa Reservoir, which can be seen for miles.

From Gunnison, it's a no-sweat flight to Montrose which, on this route, should take the place of Grand Junction as a fuel stop. Making allowances for the various detours, we will fly about 220 nm, and after fueling the airplane, defueling the pilot, and having a cup of coffee, we should still have ample time to continue.

Now a decision must be made. Using Victor airways (V-244 to V-8 to V-8N) offers the advantage of continuous contact with appropriately placed VORs. However, except for the Bryce Canyon area, it is scenically pretty dull, so, if we want to see some scenery, the thing to do is leave Montrose on the 240-degree radial and fly to Canyonlands National Park (90.4 nm), then take up a heading of 220 degrees and fly over the entire length of Lake Powell, which brings us at its western shore to Page (113 nm). From there we can follow the Colorado River south through Marble Canyon toward the Grand Canyon and then head west to Lake Mead and Las Vegas (between 220 and 260 nm). The Victor Airway route totals 388 nm, while the scenic route adds up to approximately 435 nm, give or take a few.

Now the sensible thing to do is quit for the day. Any pilot new to the Rockies should by now have his fill of scenic splendor, coupled with gradually but constantly increasing turbulence. Although the mountains ahead can't hold a candle to those behind, late-afternoon turbulence over the rest of the route will get a lot worse, rather than better.

On the charts, the flight from Las Vegas to San Diego doesn't look like much. The highest mountains along the way only go up to 7,500 feet, and the whole thing looks like a piece of cake. It isn't. The distance via Goffs, Twentynine Palms, Thermal, and Julian VORs is only 235 nm, but much of it is desert, where the heat of the day produces wind and turbulence, which can be upsetting, to pick a rather unfortunate phrase.

Again, if we can tear ourselves away from the excitement of Las Vegas, we should leave at the earliest possible hour. If not, just tighten the seatbelt, relax, and pretend it's a roller coaster.

A word of warning: non-instrument-rated pilots should be sure and check the San Diego weather. Low clouds and fog are a frequent occurrence, and it would be depressing to have come all this way and then not be able to land at the desired destination.

The total route that has been described here includes some of the most rugged and, at the same time, beautiful terrain to be found in the country. The problems mentioned are typical of those you might encounter when flying anywhere in the mountains. But simply planning the route carefully and knowing the altitudes at which to fly and the most convenient fuel stops is only one portion of what's necessary to be safe. What follows is a kind of mountain-flying checklist.

AIRCRAFT AND INSTRUMENTS

The importance of range and service ceiling has been mentioned. Note also that the *service ceiling* is not the absolute ceiling of the airplane. It is the altitude at which the aircraft, at gross weight, will still climb at 100 fpm. It will continue to climb at a constantly decreasing rate until a combination of full throttle, the right mixture, and a flight attitude approximating the best angle of climb will produce only level flight. That is its *absolute ceiling*.

Rate of climb is another parameter that takes on greater importance in the mountains. Normally most of us climb at what we consider a comfortable rate and angle, little concerned about the time and distance it takes to get to the desired altitude. In the mountains, when flying up toward a ridge or the saddle of a pass, you have to know with certainty that you can get there in time, which means knowing how many feet per minute you can squeeze out of that airframe-engine combination under the prevailing temperature conditions.

Pilots flying light twins should remember that most are incapable of maintaining the necessary altitude on one engine, and in the event of an engine malfunction, the most immediate problem will be to somehow head toward lower ground.

Takeoffs and landings on warm or hot days at high-altitude airports are something that must be experienced to be believed. The effects of density altitude are described in the next chapter.

In addition to the usual nav/comm equipment, an ADF can be helpful. It is not at all unusual to be out of VOR reception distance for long stretches of time, but there is almost always a standard broadcast station somewhere to help give you some idea of your progress.

An EGT takes on an increased value when virtually all flying is done at altitudes that require intelligent mixture control.

One instrument rarely found in light aircraft but worth its weight in gold—especially in the mountains—is an *angle-of-attack indicator*. It is simply a needle that indicates whether the attitude of the aircraft is right for climb, cruise, or descent relative to the airspeed, and it warns of approaching stalls. Mountain flying involves getting misleading cues from sloping terrain and horizons, and one is easily seduced into thinking that the attitude of the aircraft is different from what it really is. Flying the needle of an angle-of-attack indicator eliminates all that. Because it is not affected by density altitude, it produces reliable indications at all times.

Fig. 6-1. *A narrow cloud bank obscuring a ridge might cause you to climb to oxygen altitudes.*

Another item to be considered is oxygen. Quite aside from the legalities involved, prolonged high-altitude flying without supplementary oxygen might result in severe headaches at best or, at worst, in a loss of efficiency and increasing degrees of disorientation. In other words, not having oxygen is just plain stupid (although not having it while flying at altitude serves to make you more stupid).

Although a planned mountain flight might not include altitudes above 12,500 feet, you never know what conditions you might encounter. A narrow cloud bank obscuring a ridge, uncomfortable turbulence, or even just continuing updrafts might cause you to climb into oxygen altitudes, and, for this reason, you should seriously consider having at least a small portable oxygen system (FIG. 6-1).

WEATHER

Weather in the mountains is different. Visibilities are usually considerable—70 miles or more not unusual—and haze and fog conditions the rare exception because the industrial pollution enveloping much of the country is absent. As a result, distances tend to be underestimated. You'll look at a mountain or other landmark that seems quite near and then wonder why it seems to take forever to get there.

Thunderstorms build regularly during the afternoon hours in summer and fall (and sometimes spring and winter). They rarely combine into squall lines, but usually rise to impressive heights in solitary splendor. As elsewhere, they produce vicious winds, rain, and hail and must be avoided at all cost. Circumventing them is rarely a problem, assuming there is ample fuel on board for the additional miles resulting from the detour.

Small, fast-moving weather systems might develop between reporting stations and, therefore, remain unannounced. Try to circumvent, rather than over- or underfly, them. Overflying a cloud deck of any consequence can turn into a sucker trap (FIG. 6-2). From below, the tops tend to look reasonable enough, but once up there, they often continue to rise and rise until they exceed the climb capability of the airplane.

Fig. 6-2. *In the mountains, overflying a cloud deck can be a sucker trap.*

Fig. 6-3. *Always be aware that the lower clouds might be full of rocks.*

Then what? You can either turn back (unless, of course, the clouds behind you have climbed, too), or file for instruments. Or you can simply—and illegally—punch through, hoping to come out in the clear on the other end. In addition to being illegal, however, it's worse here than in flat country because you can't come down if you find you have to. You must always be aware that the lower clouds might just be full of rocks—*cumulo granite*.

Conversely, underflying such a cloud deck, unless it's distinctly clear of the ridges ahead, also can result in a dead end—literally, as well as figuratively (FIG. 6-3). In situations where clouds obscure mountaintops but a pass ahead seems clear, don't fly through the pass unless you know a way out of the next valley or there is an airport at which you can land.

WIND

Wind direction and velocity are affected by the configuration of the mountain ranges. This subject was covered in chapter 4.

NIGHT

Forget night flying, unless and until you're an experienced mountain pilot. Nothing is as black as a moonless night in that clear, hazeless air over endless stretches of uninhabited rock. By the time the mountain ahead comes into view, it might be too late to avoid it.

In summary, mountain flying can be a breathtaking and satisfying experience, but it is not to be taken lightly. Sloppy technique, slipshod preplanning, or inadequate maintenance of the aircraft, its systems, and instruments can easily make a first mountain flight the last. But planning, caution, and respect for the terrain and for its weather keep mountain pilots flying year in and year out, and there's no reason for proficient pilots from other parts of the country not to join their number.

In closing, any aircraft owner who expects to have to cross the Rockies with any degree of frequency would be well advised to consider installing a turbocharger and a permanent oxygen system. Then he can simply climb to an altitude that keeps him safely above all obstructions.

7
Precipitation

PRECIPITATION COMES IN A VARIETY OF FORMS, SOME QUITE HARMLESS; others to be avoided at all cost. Each form of precipitation presents a different set of circumstances for the pilot to cope with, whether harmless or to be avoided.

RAIN

Light drizzle or steady rain is of no particular consequence, except that it might reduce forward visibility to a degree and reveal the apparently unavoidable fact that most light aircraft cockpits tend to leak eventually. In aircraft with carbureted engines, it might be a good idea to apply carburetor heat because moisture can produce carburetor icing, no matter what the outside air temperature.

Heavy downpours are a different story. They might effectively reduce the forward visibility to a fraction of a mile, not to mention the unpleasant noise, which tends to sound like a machine gun firing at the windshield. For aircraft with carbureted engines, the same caution applies as mentioned in the last paragraph. Otherwise the aircraft won't feel any ill effects from heavy rain, although paint has been known to peel off in spots. But, discretion being the better part of valor, it is best to detour around such showers.

If the downpour comes out of the bottom of a thunderstorm, it is strictly a place to stay far away from. Not only is the area of precipitation the most likely to contain repeated lightning strikes, it probably will also be extremely turbulent. There is always the possibility that some of the rain might turn to hail large enough to severely damage the aircraft.

FREEZING RAIN

In the winter pilots often run into situations where the air aloft is comfortably above freezing, but the air below hovers around the 32°F level. If rain starts falling from above, it might turn into freezing rain when it hits the lower, colder air, or it might simply turn to ice when it hits the metal of the airplane. Either way, it can coat an aircraft with a sufficiently thick layer of ice to impair its ability to carry all that additional weight. The stall speed rises rapidly, while the TAS is gradually reduced, eventually making a descent and landing inevitable.

Depending on the degree of precipitation, this sort of thing can develop within minutes. Therefore, whenever freezing rain is even a possibility, it is a lot wiser to abandon the flight plan than to wait and see in hopes that it might not develop at all.

HAIL

Hail is never something to take lightly. It is produced by supercooled air within thunderstorms, but often falls several miles from the storm itself, usually out of the overhanging anvil clouds. Such hail has been known to attain the size of golfballs, and when it hits the leading edges of an aircraft wing or the fuselage, it can dent the surfaces to a point that airworthiness is reduced to nil. Subsequent repairs can run into astronomical figures. At the first indication of hail, a hasty retreat is the only sensible action.

SNOW

Snow can be dry or wet. Dry snow presents no danger to an aircraft, but visibility can be reduced to near zero and, especially at night, the visual effect of the stuff coming at you is extremely disconcerting and might eventually produce a degree of vertigo.

Wet snow is likely to adhere to the aircraft and freeze into ice, similar to freezing rain. In addition, it might cover the windshield to a point that is beyond the capability of the defroster to deal with, totally robbing the pilot of all forward visibility.

When there is snow on the ground, it affects takeoffs and landings. A thin layer of snow, while reducing the rate of acceleration somewhat during the takeoff run, is not a serious problem. But the drag produced by a heavy layer—3 or more inches—might double or even triple the distance needed to attain flying speed. Heavy or wet snow might cause such sudden deceleration upon touchdown that nosegear damage or even a noseover occurs. If you must make a landing in relatively deep snow, you should handle it as a short-field landing with the nosewheel held off the surface as long as possible.

FRONTS

An understanding of how and why fronts are formed, how they move, and what kinds of weather are usually associated with them is of less importance to the VFR pilot than to the IFR pilot because the VFR pilot is supposed to fly where he can see the weather. Still, it doesn't hurt to have at least some idea of how all this weather business functions.

If the air everywhere were of the same temperature and moisture content, there would be no wind and, in turn, no weather. But the atmosphere around us is punctured by low-pressure and high-pressure areas, around which the air circulates in predictable directions. Each low-pressure area is normally associated with two so-called *fronts*: a cold front and a warm front.

Differences between Warm and Cold Fronts

A front consists of a sloping transition zone between two air masses of differing temperature and moisture content. A *warm front* is formed when warm air replaces cold air at ground level and slopes upward over the cold wedge. When cold air displaces warm air at ground level, it is referred to as a *cold front*.

The slope of an active cold front is usually significantly greater than that of a warm front. In practice, this means that high clouds in advance of a warm front might appear many hundreds of miles ahead of the front itself, while advance clouds indicating a cold front appear at only relatively short distances ahead of the front.

However, cold fronts tend to move faster than warm fronts, and the fast-moving nose of the cold front forces warm air upward quite violently, resulting in strong winds and convective squalls. In short, cold fronts are usually associated with quite violent weather, winds, and turbulence, while warm fronts are fairly calm, with light winds and little turbulence.

The other difference is that warm fronts often cover large areas and might stay around for a long time, while cold fronts are smaller in area and move on quickly. In either case, depending on the moisture content of the air, the extent of the cloud formations may vary horizontally and especially vertically. With ample moisture available, cold fronts may build cumulonimbus clouds, which can attain altitudes of 30,000 feet or more. Excessive moisture in association with a warm front will increase the horizontal, rather than vertical, formation of clouds.

Rain Areas

Both kinds of fronts will usually involve rain. The rain area of a warm front can extend for hundreds of miles, while the rain associated with a cold front might be heavier, but is usually restricted to much smaller areas. Figures 7-1 and 7-2 show the typical profiles of such fronts, while FIG. 7-3 illustrates the typical position of fronts with relation to the low in the early, middle, and latter stages.

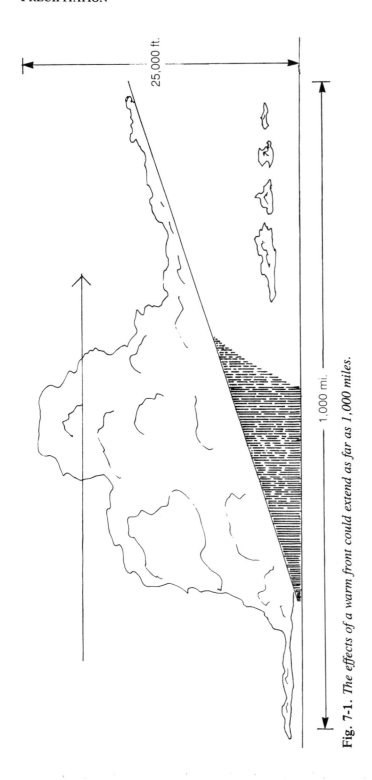

Fig. 7-1. The effects of a warm front could extend as far as 1,000 miles.

25,000 ft.

1,000 mi.

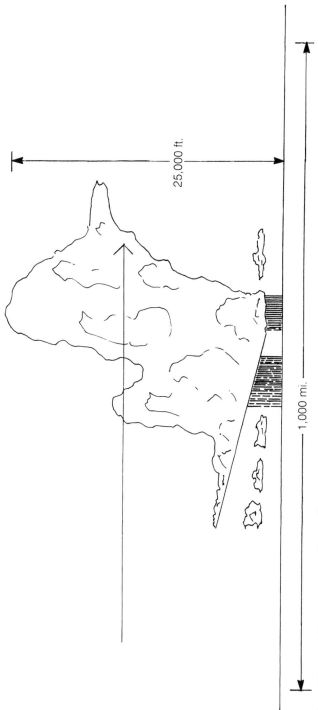

Fig. 7-2. *Cold fronts are usually smaller in area, but more violent.*

25,000 ft.

1,000 mi.

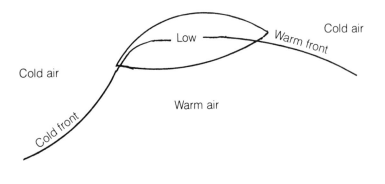

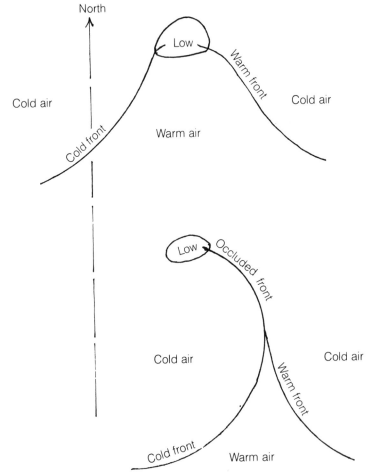

Fig. 7-3. *Low-pressure areas are associated with a warm and a cold front.*

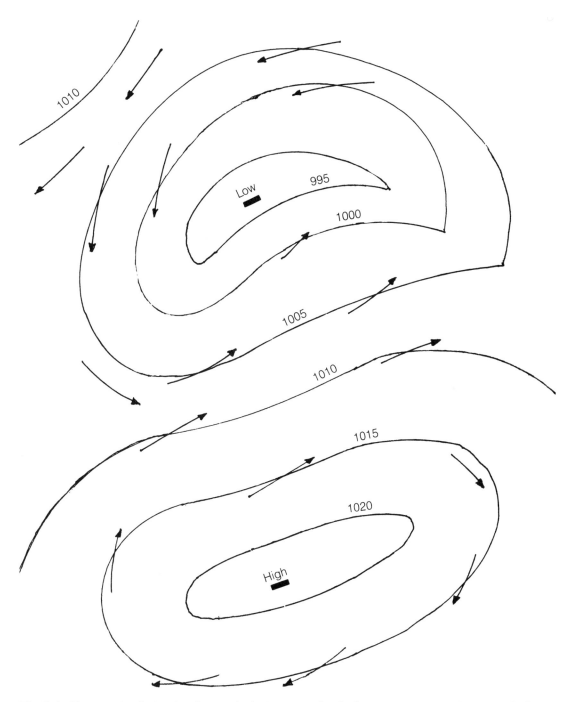

Fig. 7-4. *The air circulation is always clockwise around a high-pressure area and counterclockwise around a low-pressure area.*

Since the airflow around highs and lows is consistently the same—clockwise, or *anticyclone*, around a high, and counterclockwise, or *cyclone*, around a low (FIG. 7-4)—knowing the position of high- and low-pressure areas can be helpful in planning a course that will take advantage of favorable winds.

WEATHER CHARTS

The VFR pilot who takes the trouble to become familiar with weather charts and learns what all those hieroglyphics mean, and then who takes the additional trouble to go to the nearest FSS to look at current weather charts, will start on his cross-country flight knowing where to expect weather and how to avoid the worst headwinds. Figure 7-5 is a typical weather chart covering all of the contiguous United States.

Now let's say that a pilot wants to fly from El Paso, Texas, to Pierre, South Dakota. The straight line would take him right through the middle of a low-pressure system with quartering headwinds most of his route. By crossing over to the other side of the cold front, which lies more or less along the border between Texas and New Mexico and which, according to the chart, does not have any significant precipitation associated with it, he can take advantage of strong tailwinds (30 to 35 kts) all the way into Nebraska.

In Nebraska, he'll encounter that same cold front once more, and a small area of active precipitation is indicated between North Platte and Pierre, but he will probably be able to fly around it, and the winds will still be helping him, rather than holding him back. In terms of distance, the straight-line route is approximately 800 nm, while the detour around the low would add another 125 nm.

Assuming that the airplane being flown cruises at 130 kts, the straight-line route would take 6 hours and 9 minutes under no-wind conditions, but with the winds indicated on the chart, it would take something like 7 hours and 40 minutes. The longer route, under no-wind conditions, would take 7 hours and 7 minutes. With the tailwind component shown on the chart, it would take 5 hours and 45 minutes. In addition, it is likely to be a smoother, and therefore more pleasant, flight, with the possible exception of the two times when the cold front has to be crossed.

As a general rule, most VFR pilots (and most IFR pilots, for that matter) don't bother with detailed studies of the weather charts, which are available in all Flight Service Stations. Practically the only time we bother with them is when the weather along our proposed route of flight is forecast to be bad, and even then we are likely to depend on and accept the interpretation given by the flight service specialist. The trouble is that no matter how helpful these fellows might try to be, most of them are not pilots, and even if they are, they can't possibly know our capabilities and the capability of our airplane.

Taking the lazy way out and accepting the specialist's judgment that a flight can or cannot be made VFR is no way to go about flight planning. All decisions made with reference to a flight, whether before takeoff or while in the air, are in the final analysis, the sole responsibility of the pilot in command.

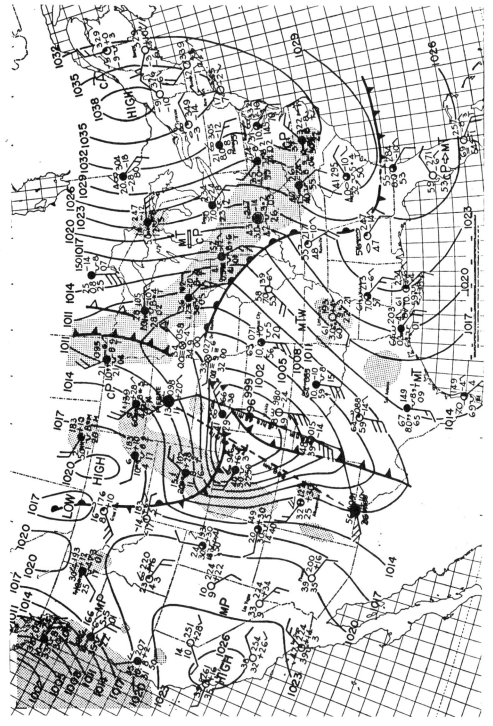

Fig. 7-5. By studying the weather charts, you can take advantage of favorable winds.

In most instances, when a pilot finds himself confronted by unexpected marginal or worse weather conditions, it is because of sloppy preplanning. Granted, weather forecasts are frequently unreliable. Time and again you will find that it's either much better or much worse than it is supposed to be. However, by carefully examining the current conditions along your proposed route and within 50 to 100 miles to either side of that route, you frequently can devise your own estimate as to the conditions you are likely to encounter.

The more you know of the conditions all around you before starting on a flight—and every minute during the flight—the less your chances of running into something you can't handle safely and legally.

ICE IS FOR COCKTAILS

The pilot of the Comanche had been the victim of his own optimism. Impatient with scooting around under a low broken overcast and detouring around intermittent showers, he had climbed to VFR conditions on top and now found himself at 12,500 feet above St. Louis.

The trouble was that the broken clouds had long ago coalesced into a solid deck (FIG. 7-6). And he was due in St. Louis within the next few hours. Lambert Field was reporting 800 ft. overcast with 3 miles' visibility in light rain. Well, instrument ticket

Fig. 7-6. *Soon the sky above and the sun were disappearing.*

or no, he'd either have to file and descend through this stuff or go elsewhere and forget about getting to St. Louis on time.

He felt confident that he could make the approach under the reported conditions, so he called St. Louis FSS and filed IFR to Lambert. A short time later he was told to expect vectors to an ILS approach to Runway 12R.

"Radar contact. Descend to and maintain 6,000. Report passing through ten and eight, report reaching six. Maintain present heading."

The pilot acknowledged, reduced power, and set up a comfortable rate of descent. By the time all the blue sky and the sun above had disappeared, he had successfully forced himself to stop paying attention to the outside and instead concentrated on his instruments. He felt certain that he would be able to follow ATC instructions and that, with an 800-foot ceiling and 3-mile visibility, he would be able to land safely, even though he had never actually flown an ILS approach.

The first indication that something wasn't quite the way it should be came when he found that he had difficulty receiving ATC on his radio. Transmissions kept breaking up, and several times he had to ask for three or more repetitions to make sure that he had understood correctly what he was being asked to do. He made a mental note to have his radio checked the first chance he got.

The second indication was more subtle. Somehow the airplane didn't feel quite right. It seemed to be in an awful hurry to lose altitude, and it didn't seem right to have to add power in order to maintain the desired rate of descent. And holding altitude required nearly full power with an uncomfortable nose-high attitude.

Although based in Southern California where icing in clouds is not a routine occurrence, the pilot had by now figured out that he was picking up ice. Never having had this happen to him before, he was unaware of the rapidity with which ice tends to form when the temperature and humidity are just right, and he, therefore, did not tell ATC what was happening.

As it turned out, he was relatively lucky. ATC cleared him to descend from 6,000 feet without much delay, and once passing through 4,000 the outside air temperature climbed to comfortably above freezing. By the time he broke out of the clouds with Runway 12R right over his nose, the airplane was behaving normally again and the radio reception was as it should be. Once stopped on the ramp, there was no indication anywhere of the amount of ice the airplane must have been carrying only a few minutes earlier.

ICING

It is too bad that pilots rarely get an opportunity to actually see what an iced-up airplane looks like in flight. No spoken or printed warning could ever expect to scare us the way the real thing would. In this particular incident, the initial reception difficulties were caused by ice buildup around the VHF antenna. This used to be more serious with the older type of antennas, but the new streamlined varieties are less prone to ice accumulation.

The airplane itself tends to attract ice wherever there are protrusions, such as rivet heads and metal seams. And ice likes to adhere to ice, so as soon as a tiny bit has formed near one of those metal irregularities, it is likely to grow and spread quickly.

The resulting performance deterioration can be quite drastic. Ice is heavy, and this kind usually results in a rough surface, which plays havoc with an airfoil. Thus, as more ice adheres, the angle of attack must be increased in order to maintain level flight, thus exposing more and more of the underside of the airplane to the slipstream, which usually is less clean than the upper surfaces and thus prone to accelerate ice accumulation. Because the ice is in areas that the pilot cannot see, his only means of guessing what is happening is in the way the aircraft handles.

Visible Moisture

For ice to be able to form in the first place, there must be what is referred to as *visible moisture*: clouds, freezing rain, or haze with an extremely high humidity content. The outside air temperature most conducive to ice formation ranges from about 33° or 34° down to 22° to 24°F. Once it gets colder than that, the moisture is already frozen and is not likely to adhere to the aircraft.

As we all know, temperatures vary with altitude. Usually it gets colder the higher we go, but under certain conditions it might be colder near the ground and warmer higher up. Those who are experts at reading weather charts can figure out which situation is likely to occur where, but the fact is that most of us aren't expert. Also, when we need the charts, they usually don't happen to be handy.

The reason for wanting to know what is happening with the temperature above and below is the need to make a decision quickly, to climb or descend when you are in an area where ice is forming. What you are looking for is either a level of warmer air that will permit the ice to melt, or much colder air, which is most often found in clear VFR conditions above. Once in the colder air, the ice gradually will dissipate through evaporation.

In making such an up or down decision, you also must take under consideration the ability of the aircraft to climb speedily to the desired altitude with whatever load of ice has already accumulated, plus whatever additional amount it will pick up during the climb. If the aircraft is one that, under these conditions, is still able to achieve an honest 500 fpm rate of climb, fine. If, on the other hand, the best that can be coaxed from the airplane is a dawdling 150 or 200 fpm, it might be better to start looking for some place lower down because the airplane is likely to arrive at a point at which it will barely maintain level flight before it gets to the adequately cold altitude above.

VFR pilots are, of course, not supposed to find themselves in icing conditions. But what is supposed to be and what actually does happen are often two different things. It is, therefore, important to at least know where ice might be found and what to do when it is found.

Types of Icing

So far we have talked about icing in relation to the airframe and to aircraft performance. There are other types of icing that, although not exactly in the same classification, do deserve to be talked about.

Carburetor Ice. Somehow carburetor ice never seems to have been comprehended particularly well, and with an increasing number of today's new engines being fuel injected, both encountering it and understanding it are likely to become even more obscure.

First of all, carburetor icing is possible in the middle of summer on a hot, humid day. It has little if anything to do with the outside air temperature. What happens is that while going through the carburetor, the air reaches a point called the *venturi*, where the carburetor throat widens out. As you might know, when air is compressed, its temperature rises. Conversely, as it expands—as it does after passing the venturi—its temperature drops. In a carburetor, the air cools rapidly to such a point that if there is moisture present, it is likely to freeze.

This situation usually occurs when the temperature and dew point are only a few degrees apart. The moisture can freeze into clumps, which adhere to the intake orifice, resulting in a slow and sure choking of engine air. So, whenever you notice a gradual unexplained reduction in the power of a carbureted engine, pull the carburetor heat control all the way out. Unless you have waited too long, the heat will melt the ice and after a bit of spitting and coughing, the engine will regain near-normal power. It won't be full power because the preheated air alters the fuel-air relationship and reduces the amount of power available.

If you anticipate prolonged operation with carburetor heat, you should relean the engine. The correct routine is to continue to fly with carburetor heat full on as long as the conditions of excessive moisture remain present. Never use partial carburetor heat; like being pregnant, it's all or nothing.

Frozen Rain. Another ice-related problem is one that is rarely serious, but can be quite unpleasant. Here is what can happen: you take off in the rain, maintain a steady rate of climb, and eventually arrive in clear conditions above the clouds. You now try to trim the airplane for level flight, except it won't trim. The trim tab, soaked from the rain, froze as you climbed to a below-freezing altitude and now it's stuck, and it's not going to come loose again until you get back down to where it's warmer.

Solution? Either you fly the entire way to your destination pushing like mad on the yoke in order to keep the nose down, or you throttle back to some sort of slow-flight speed that will keep the airplane level in that nose-high attitude, or you go back down until the thing comes loose and then climb back up, exercising the trim tab and, possibly, the other controls repeatedly in order to avoid having them freeze on you again.

There are extreme cases on record where the primary controls—elevator, rudder, and ailerons—froze as the result of a similar situation. If that should happen, the only sensible solution is to throttle back and let the airplane settle back down until the controls start to work again.

A variation on the theme would be frozen flaps. This situation could be scary, especially in an airplane with hydraulic or electric flap actuators, because they might bend or tear something, possibly ending up with one flap down and one up, a situation that has been known to kill people.

Iced Pitot Tube. Still another icing condition to watch for is what can occur when there is moisture in the pitot tube and you climb to below-freezing temperatures. The moisture will freeze and all airspeed indication will be lost. If the aircraft is equipped with pitot heat, that will usually take care of it. Always use pitot heat as a preventive measure under such conditions.

If no pitot heat is available, there is nothing you can do. You simply have to fly without an airspeed indication, which is actually not as difficult as it might seem.

Similarly, when flying an aircraft equipped with a gear-lowering device that is operated by air pressure into a pitot-tubelike gadget, the air intake can freeze over and suddenly the gear will come down unannounced. Unless you are cruising at an excessively high speed, this is not likely to do the gear any harm, but the gear doors, being more fragile, could be bent or actually torn off.

It should not be necessary to state that taking off in an airplane with any amount of ice, snow, or even frost on the wings, tail surfaces, or fuselage is extremely dangerous. One wonders how often those famous last words, "Oh, that isn't enough to mean anything," have been spoken a short time before a fatal crash. Admittedly, it is a nuisance to drag an airplane into a heated hangar to let it thaw out and dry off or to spend a half hour or more in freezing wind with a broom trying to clean away the last remnants of last night's snowstorm, but that's just the name of the game, and if you want to play it safe, that's what you had better do.

8
Storms

THE LONGER YOU FLY, THE GREATER ARE YOUR CHANCES OF OCCASIONALLY rubbing elbows with what might be referred to as severe weather. Early in your flying career, you might make a firm decision never to fly when the weather looks somewhat doubtful. But as you pile up more hours, you soon realize that if you want to restrict your flying activity strictly to CAVU (ceiling and visibility unlimited) weather, you'll be using your airplane a lot less than is necessary in order to justify your investment in flight instruction and, of course, the airplane itself.

THUNDERSTORMS

The most frequent kind of severe weather, some contact with which is virtually unavoidable, is the thunderstorm (FIG. 8-1). Like most weather phenomena, thunderstorms come in a variety of shapes and sizes, but they all have one thing in common. Inside, they are murderous, capable of tearing an airplane to pieces, and must therefore be avoided at all cost.

The easiest type of thunderstorm to deal with is the so-called *airmass thunderstorm*. With its "anvil" top, it usually stands alone in solitary splendor, surrounded by clear skies and unrestricted visibility. It can be seen for miles, and as a result, course adjustments can be made early to give it a wide berth. Whenever possible, you should plan a detour around these storms for the side away from the direction of the anvil

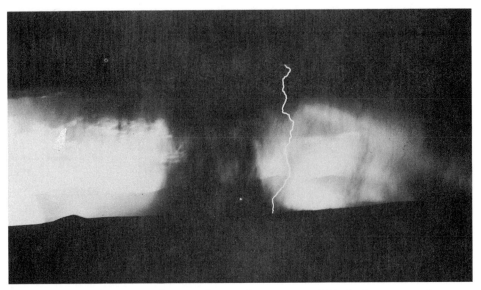

Fig. 8-1. *A thunderstorm is the most frequently encountered kind of severe weather.*

Fig. 8-2. *Embedded thunderstorms often cannot be seen and are, therefore, hard to avoid.*

cloud. Although this anvil, which might be as high as 40,000 feet, might seem perfectly harmless, there is always the chance that hail might spew from it, and hail is something that airplanes are not designed to deal with.

The worst type of thunderstorm from the point of view of a pilot is the *embedded* variety because, more often than not, it cannot be seen, and as a result you don't know that you're about to fly into it unless you're already on top of it (FIG. 8-2). But since they are embedded in solid IFR weather, they should not be of consequence to the VFR pilot because there is no excuse for that pilot to be in that kind of weather in the first place. IFR pilots, unless they are flying airplanes equipped with weather radar, have little choice but to rely on information provided by ground-based radar and the ability of the ATC controller to vector them around the most intense areas of these storms.

The third variety encountered with any frequency is the *squall line*, a long line of individual storms often stretching hundreds of miles and 20 or 30 miles in width (FIG. 8-3). Occasionally there might be sufficiently wide spaces between individual cells to permit penetration of such a line, but there will always be considerable turbulence and the danger of encountering hail. Most of us have flown through such openings between storms at one time or another, but it is neither comfortable nor a procedure to be recommended. If you are high, there might be a place where the tops of the clouds are low enough to make it possible to stay in VFR conditions on top. This is described in greater detail in another chapter.

Fig. 8-3. *A sharply defined squall line of thunderstorms often can extend for hundreds of miles.*

WIND SHEAR

One aviation nemesis getting a lot of attention is wind shear associated with thunderstorm downbursts of air. Encountering a downburst at the wrong time under the wrong circumstances, such as low and slow during an approach, spells doom for any airplane, large or small. Remember that downbursts are in thunderstorms. Avoid a thunderstorm and you avoid the downburst.

A *downburst* is a short-lived powerful rush of air that descends perpendicular to the surface of the earth, almost always in a thunderstorm. When it encounters the ground, it spreads out in all directions, creating turbulent air that wreaks havoc with an airplane.

Initially the airplane will experience a strong headwind, slowing its ground speed; then a powerful downdraft forces the airplane down, followed immediately by a strong tailwind that dramatically increases the ground speed. However, it is airspeed that keeps an airplane flying, and the sudden switch from headwind to tailwind usually leaves the airplane without enough airspeed to stay airborne. In addition, an airplane on approach will already be low, slow, and "dirty," with landing gear, flaps, and/or speed brakes extended. An unsuspecting pilot might have a hard time dealing with the fast-changing situation and be unable to control the airplane.

Detecting downbursts within a thunderstorm requires Doppler radar to measure the velocity and direction of particles in the air, primarily rain drops. (Despite the wider safety margin offered by Doppler radar, the installation schedule will be driven by governmental economies, first appearing at major airports and spreading to others when feasible.)

Using Doppler, meteorologists and air traffic control personnel will be able to locate wind shear and downbursts and to warn pilots of its presence. Pilots can then elect to deviate or penetrate the turbulence. Properly prepared, an airplane might fly safely through it. The more prudent choice would be to abandon the maneuver—like an approach to a landing—and try again when the turbulence has subsided.

TORNADOES AND HURRICANES

In certain parts of the country, thunderstorm activity can be associated with the development of tornadoes. In other areas, hurricanes are an unpleasant fact of life. When a tornado or hurricane is even suspected, retreat is the only sensible course. Luckily our airplanes fly a lot faster than these storms move, so there is never the danger of being overrun by one from behind.

This is true, of course, of all kinds of weather. It is physically impossible for weather to catch up with an airplane. Whenever a pilot gets into bad weather, it is the pilot who did the catching up, not the weather system. Anyone who claims that he found himself inadvertently in weather is stretching the truth. Granted, the weather into which he flew might have been worse than anticipated, but the pilot certainly did know in advance that he was flying into conditions of which he might have had no way of determining the severity.

DUST DEVILS

Mini-tornadoes, or so-called *dust devils*, usually look relatively harmless, but they can be quite lethal. I have seen one pick up an airplane sitting on the ground, lift it into the air, then toss it back, breaking a lot of expensive structure in the process.

Dust devils rarely extend upwards to altitudes in excess of a few thousand feet, but whenever you spot one below along your course, it is always a better idea to detour around it, rather than to take a chance on having it make a grab for the airplane. And it goes without saying that, when you suspect dust devil activity, you should tie down aircraft on the ground securely.

SANDSTORMS

One of the least attractive—although not necessarily dangerous—weather phenomena is the dust or sandstorm. They occur most frequently in the desert areas of the Southwest, although they occasionally develop elsewhere, such as on areas of large, unprotected farmland.

You can be flying along in perfectly good VFR conditions when you gradually become aware of a reduction in visibility and, most probably, an increase in turbulence. The air might take on a yellowish or grayish tinge and the ground might be barely visible. You might want to climb higher in order to get on top of the mess, but many of these storms will top 15,000 feet, making the attempt fruitless. There isn't much you can do except keep on flying, primarily by instruments, and hope that you can be out of it soon.

Sand or dust storms are bad for the engine, and if you're flying an aircraft with a ram-air intake—such as a Mooney—the intake should be closed.

Because most such storms are generated by strong surface winds, they act much like smoke, meaning that they are relatively narrow but might extend for great distances downwind from their source. In order to minimize the time during which you expose yourself and the engine to the dust-laden air, it is a good idea to figure out the direction of the wind and then fly at right angles to it, rather than into or downwind of it. Even if such a change of direction results in a detour, it is preferable to flying in the storm for a prolonged period of time. If worse comes to worst, a landing might be the ticket. An hour or two on the ground might be all that is needed to allow the storm to dissipate.

Sometimes these storms—especially sandstorms—are clearly defined, making it relatively easy to fly around the cloud of sand and dust. More often than not, however, they tend to sneak up on you, and when that happens the only choice is to either relax and try to enjoy it or to make a 180, land, and wait. Dropping down to a lower altitude, as you normally would do in order to stay below an overcast, is rarely of use. In practically all cases, these storms extend from the ground up, and conditions at low altitudes are likely to be a great deal worse than higher up.

After flying through a bad dust storm, it is a good idea to drop in at the nearest FBO and have him change the oil. Although this procedure won't remove all the grit and crud, it will take care of a lot of it, and your engine will be grateful in the long run.

DASTARDLY DUST

Two pilots had to make a 300-mile, cross-country trip. They departed midmorning, stopped halfway to conduct business, and continued later that afternoon for home. Although one of the pilots owned the airplane, the flight was supposed to be a familiarization for the other pilot to build time in the airplane to satisfy insurance requirements. As luck would have it, he not only would become familiar with the airplane, but learn about flying in a dust storm as well.

Takeoff

A brown western sky made it obvious that weather would be a factor on the trip, and the two discussed who would take the left seat. The plane's owner was instrument-rated and much more familiar with the airplane, but the other pilot needed the hours. The first destination was reporting a dust storm, but was still VFR, so the new pilot took the left seat with an IFR copilot.

After takeoff, it was obvious that the dust storm was getting worse. Climbing through the brown air, they lost sight of the ground at several thousand feet. Hoping to get on top of the dust cloud, they climbed to 10,500, found that the tint extended even higher, and leveled off—surrounded by dark brown below and a dingy blue-brown sky above.

"Could you handle this on your own?" the copilot queried.

"No," the pilot said, shaking his head. "I would have stayed home until tomorrow."

"Well, this is a good demonstration of the value of an instrument rating," the copilot continued. "With it we can do our business and be home for supper tonight. Otherwise we would be stuck waiting for the weather to clear."

A Safe Port in Any Storm . . .

Two airports were available for the stop-over: one with a single, narrow, north-south runway, with VOR, NDB, and radar approaches; another with several long and wide runways and an ILS. The smaller airport would be more convenient to the business meeting, but the larger airport would be safer because of size and precision approach facilities. They chose the latter.

The copilot called approach control and requested an IFR clearance to land. ATC complied with the request and vectored the flight around the airport. They were assisting a solo cross-country student pilot w. o had underestimated the power of the storm. As it turned out, the student landed safe. ' and did not interrupt airport operations.

The VFR pilot flew ATC's vectors while the IFR copilot familiarized himself with the approach. Prior to initiating the approach, the copilot took the controls. As clouds of dirt moved across the airport, conditions would change rapidly from VFR to IFR. Approaching the airport, on the localizer, the pilots hoped it would be VFR so they could land on a runway that pointed directly into the 20- to 40-knot wind.

However, with the approach lights in sight (it was that dark in the dust storm), the airport went IFR, forcing a 45-degree crosswind landing on the main runway. Crabbing into the wind, the copilot flew the airplane to just above the runway, pulled the power back, straightened it over the center stripe, and landed.

Homeward Bound

There was no rush to complete their business. The dust storm seemed to be letting up, and every hour they waited meant better flying conditions on departure. Sure enough, visibility improved, so the second leg could be conducted VFR, but the dust was still present, and they would face a fiendish headwind.

The second leg would be a night flight, and conditions could worsen without notice, so the IFR pilot/plane owner climbed into the left seat to complete the journey. It proved to be a rough and slow ride, with farm and city lights veiled by the dust.

Arriving at the uncontrolled home airport, the tetrahedron and windsock proved their worse fears were true. There were two runways—north-south and east-west—but only the former was lighted. Winds were straight out of the west at probably more than 30 kts. Fortunately, the plane's owner had operated from the airport for several years and knew the other runway's exact location.

Flying a standard rectangular pattern, the pilot lined up for what appeared to be a landing in a pasture. On cue, the east-west runway appeared under the landing light, and he touched down without incident on the centerline.

Winds subsided overnight to a morning calm, but it would take several days for the tons of sand and dirt particles to settle out of the atmosphere. The airplane's oil was changed to flush out any dirt ingested during the storm.

The morning after the flight, the newer pilot stopped by a flight school at the airport and began training for his instrument license.

9
Temperature

TEMPERATURE IS AN IMPORTANT FACTOR IN AVIATION. IT AFFECTS THE WAY airplanes behave during virtually every phase of flight. Temperature creates changes in the composition of the air, and without air, airplanes couldn't fly and engines couldn't run.

Normal atmospheric conditions—those used to determine all those performance figures in the owner's manuals—are 59 °F (15 °C) at sea level. Any variation from this norm will cause variations in the manner in which the airplane flies and the engine performs. Two major components of an airplane need air to perform their functions: the airfoils and the powerplant.

The *airfoils* are the wings, horizontal and vertical stabilizers, and propeller blades. Air flowing over the wings creates lift. Air flowing over the stabilizers creates directional stability in the horizontal and vertical planes. Air pushed past the rotating propeller blades creates thrust.

The engine must be fed a mixture in an approximate proportion of 15 lbs. of air for each pound of fuel. The less air available, the less power the engine is able to produce.

DENSITY ALTITUDE

Cold air is thick; it contains more molecules than warm air. As the temperature of the air rises, its density lessens. When the number of molecules contained in a given unit of air is reduced by a higher temperature, the effect of that air on airfoils and engines is also reduced. This condition is called *density altitude* because air loses density not only with increasing temperature, but also with increasing altitude. Thus, when the temperature at sea level is around 100 °F, the conditions are equal to those at a 3,000-foot altitude, or to put it another way, a sea-level airport at 100 °F has a density altitude of 3,000 feet. And at that altitude, the maximum performance capability of the average, normally aspirated engine and the airfoils is reduced by about 20 percent. In practice, this means that an airplane requiring a takeoff run of 1,000 feet at sea level and 59 °F will require 1,200 feet with the 3,000-foot density altitude and will suffer a rate of climb also reduced by 20 percent.

One might argue that thinner air would reduce the adverse effect of drag. Although this might be true in high-flying, high-performance aircraft, the improvement in performance it provides is so minimal as to not be worth serious consideration.

THE EFFECT OF TEMPERATURE

Let's take the various phases of flight and analyze the effect of temperature. It is probably most serious during takeoff, especially if it is at a high-altitude airport (FIG. 9-1). The greater the temperature, the longer the airplane will take to accelerate to flying speed, and once airborne, it might not achieve a decent rate of climb for an inordinately long time.

On a hot summer afternoon at a place like Denver, with its 5,000-foot-plus elevation, the density altitude might be 8,000 feet or more, which is only a few thousand feet below the service ceiling of many smaller single-engine aircraft and some of the older twins.

Fig. 9-1. *The effects of temperature are most serious during takeoff, especially if it is at a high-altitude airport.*

Obviously, you can't expect much of a rate of climb if you start your flight close to the service ceiling in terms of density altitude. The wings don't have enough airflow to produce adequate lift, and the *manifold pressure*, the air pressure needed by the engine in order to produce power, is too low to achieve normal operation.

Airspeed Is Airspeed

Two factors are of major importance under these circumstances. One involves understanding the readings produced by the airspeed indicator.

The relationship of the indicated airspeed (IAS) to liftoff speed, stall speed, etc., does not change with density altitude. If an airplane lifts off under normal altitude and temperature conditions at, say, 65 knots IAS, it will lift off at that same speed on a hot summer day at a high-altitude airport. However, even though the IAS is the same, the true airspeed and the ground speed are much higher. The airplane does not know how fast it is going over the ground. It only reacts to how fast it is going through the air.

A pilot who is not accustomed to operating under these conditions should ignore the visual impression resulting from the great speed with which he is moving across the ground and be guided solely by the airspeed indicator to determine when he has reached takeoff or landing speeds. Conversions from IAS to TAS should be made only after a safe cruising altitude has been reached.

The other important consideration has to do with the engine. Most of us who normally operate from airports located at fairly low elevations will automatically tend to want to operate the engine at its full-rich mixture during the takeoff phase of the flight. If, however, the density altitude is high, say 5,000 feet or more, then that mixture would be too rich to permit the engine to function properly. At best, it will produce less power; at worst, it can result in spark plug fouling within minutes, which can cause the engine to sputter or actually fail at a time when such a malfunction might easily have catastrophic consequences. Therefore, the pilot should lean the mixture during the pretakeoff runup.

In aircraft equipped with an exhaust gas temperature gauge, a good rule of thumb would be to run the engine up to full throttle on the ground and lean it until the gauge reads approximately 100 degrees on the rich side of peak. That mixture setting should be used for takeoff.

On aircraft without an EGT gauge and with a fixed-pitch propeller, the mixture should be adjusted until the highest rpm is achieved with the throttle full in. The only other indicator of the proper mixture would be the sound of the engine.

On hot days, especially when there is little wind, prolonged operation of the engine on the ground can cause it to overheat rapidly. If a cylinder-head temperature (CHT) gauge is available, be sure that its indication remains in the green. Too much heat in the engine compartment is not only detrimental to the health of the engine, it also reduces the amount of power being produced. On airplanes without a CHT gauge, the oil temperature, although less reliable, will give an indication of engine temperature.

During the cruise portion of a flight, the air temperature is of less concern than during the takeoff and landing phases. If it's hotter than normal at altitude, the service ceiling and the absolute ceiling will be somewhat lower than at colder temperatures. In flat country, this will be of no great concern. In the mountains, it might mean the difference between being able to get over some high terrain or having to fly around it.

Temperature also has an effect on the altimeter readings. When it's very cold, the altimeter will read higher than you actually are. The error is not very great—some 4 percent for each 20 °F—but it can be critical when, on a cold day, you judge your ability to get over an obstacle by the reading obtained from the altimeter. In practice, if you're flying at 10,000 feet according to the altimeter and the outside air temperature is −20 °F, your actual altitude will be 9,000 feet. A simple way to remember this is that, the lower the temperature, the lower you are in relation to what the altimeter is telling you.

How to Gauge Landings

When you are coming in for a landing, the effect of high-density altitude is similar to that at takeoff, although the reasons are somewhat different. While the takeoff requires a longer than normal distance because of the reduced power available from the engine, this power availability is of no consequence when landing. However, because of the vastly increased difference between IAS and TAS, you will actually be touching down at a much higher TAS and ground speed, thus needing a lot more runway in order to slow down the airplane.

Again, in setting up your final approach speed, you should take care to ignore the speed indication received from visual clues from the outside and use the right indicated airspeed for the approach—the speed that remains unaffected by density altitude.

During the summer, when high-temperature days are the rule, rather than the exception, it is advisable to plan most flying activity for the early morning hours before the heat of the day. Not only will the airplane perform better, it is also a lot more comfortable because heat-related turbulence is at a minimum. An additional advantage is that most thunderstorm activity is generated during the afternoon and early evening.

10
Winter Flying

DEPENDING ON WHERE YOU LIVE, AS MUCH AS HALF OF THE YEAR MIGHT be winter, and if you want to keep on flying, some special precautions are necessary. Every phase of flight requires a degree of special attention: airport conditions, preflight, in-flight, and arrival all take on added dimensions. Knowing what to expect and how to combat the conditions that are encountered will help make winter flying safe and enjoyable.

AIRPORTS

During the summer over 16,000 airports and landing strips in the United States are available to the general aviation pilot. During the winter, however, quite a few of them are inoperative because snow and ice on the runways and taxiways make it impossible to use them with an adequate degree of safety.

For this reason, it is not only important to know the surface conditions at the departure airport before starting to taxi, it is also vital to be aware of the conditions expected at the destination airport at the estimated time of arrival. Furthermore, as conditions have a habit of changing rapidly and often unexpectedly, it is essential to carry at least double the fuel reserve you consider ample during the summer months, since an acceptable alternate airport might be a long distance from a destination that has suddenly gone sour.

TIEDOWNS

Subfreezing temperature causes oil to harden and batteries to weaken. It also tends to deflate landing gear struts if the aircraft flew in from a warmer climate. Strong winds might make it impossible to preheat the engine with external heater-blowers, and frequently the only way to get going is to have the FBO move the airplane into a heated hangar to get it thawed out. However, hangar space is hard to come by during the winter, and it might be necessary to make arrangements for it in advance to avoid lengthy delays.

SNOW, ICE, AND FROST

Frozen moisture, when adhering to the fuselage, wings, and tail surfaces—even in small amounts—will deform the airfoil to the degree that takeoff and subsequent flight might be dangerous, if not impossible. The aircraft must be clean to fly. Dry snow can be brushed off with a broom or rags, but frost and ice must be melted away, usually making it essential to tow the airplane into a heated hangar and leave it there until all traces of moisture have dried. Remember that moisture, once hit by the cold outside air, can freeze instantly on metal surfaces, thus defeating the purpose of having moved the airplane into the hangar in the first place.

FAST-CHANGING CONDITIONS

During the winter, weather systems and fronts tend to be fast-moving and smaller in area than in the summer. As a result, weather along the route of flight and at the destination might change drastically from hour to hour. Always keep a continuous listening watch so you are informed of current conditions ahead. Especially in mountain areas, clouds often form quite suddenly, obscuring ridges and rolling down into the

Fig. 10-1. *Clouds form quite suddenly, obscuring ridges and rolling down into the valleys.*

valleys and canyons, making continued VFR flight chancy, if not out of the question (FIG. 10-1).

Icing conditions, usually a greater hazard to IFR pilots than those operating VFR, are discussed in detail in chapter 7.

CABIN HEAT

Be sure that the cabin heater is in good working condition and that there are no leaks in the heater hoses. Sitting in an airplane with fingers and toes turning to ice can be a ghastly experience for pilot and passengers alike.

When using the heater, however, always keep some ventilation going in addition to the cabin heat. Carbon monoxide (CO) has no taste, smell, or color, and it is difficult to be absolutely certain that the exhaust manifold doesn't have a leak somewhere that could cause exhaust gases to be sucked up by the heater and channeled into the cabin. Ideally, the hot air should be directed at the feet and some cold air at the face.

There are several products on the market to detect carbon monoxide. One of the best is simply a patch of special material adhered to the dash, which changes color in the presence of CO.

AFTER DARK

Winter nights are longer than winter days; therefore, winter flying without flying at night doesn't get you very far. In some respects, VFR night flying is easier when the sky is clear and the ground is covered with snow. Roads are clearly visible as dark bands in the white landscape, even when there is no moon. Also, unlighted airports (and when there is snow, some runway lights might be buried under it) appear as dark strips against the white.

PREFLIGHT

During the winter, the preflight weather check should include questions with reference to the expected conditions of the destination airport at the estimated time of arrival. If forecasts suggest the possibility of snow, freezing rain, or a drastic drop in temperature, even if conditions are expected to be VFR, it might be advisable to telephone the destination airport to make sure that the runway will be kept clear of snow and ice. If there is any doubt, you should be prepared to use an alternate airport, preferably a major airline terminal that can be expected to have continuous clearing operations.

The next step is the actual preflight. The usual walk around should include a look inside the wheel pants on fixed-gear aircraft to make sure that no accumulations of mud or ice have frozen inside. Check fuel caps, vents, and static ports and be sure that they are free of dirt or frozen moisture, or there might be danger of collapsing a fuel tank.

Prior to starting, pull the prop through a few times to loosen the oil and thus reduce strain on the battery, which puts out less power when it's cold. Under conditions of extreme cold, an auxiliary power unit (APU) might be unavoidable. The oil will simply be too thick and the battery too weak to produce the degree of rotation necessary to get the engine to fire.

Some aircraft lubrication specialists say that a *cold start* is anything below 60 °F. Many owners opt for the advantages of multiviscosity oil in their engines to ensure easier winter starting qualities while retaining normal protection once the engine is up to operating temperatures.

If the aircraft is equipped with a constant-speed prop, exercise it more often than during warmer months. It takes a while for the oil in the mechanism to warm up and permit it to operate properly. Do not attempt to take off until the oil pressure gauge is at least in the green. On exceptionally cold days, however, the gauge might never get into the green until after the aircraft is airborne.

TAXI AND TAKEOFF

Prior to releasing the brakes, be sure you know the condition of the taxiway and runway surfaces. Frozen moisture, patches of ice, and even small amounts of snow on the ground can make taxiing difficult and might affect takeoff considerations. Ice on the ground might make a runup impossible because the brakes won't hold the aircraft in place. It might be necessary to run up the engine while the aircraft is still tied down, making sure that no debris is being blown on other aircraft behind it. Or, you might have to perform a cursory runup while taxiing.

If the runway is slippery and there is a crosswind, be prepared to slide sideways across the runway until you have obtained adequate speed. Start the takeoff run on the upwind side of the runway to avoid sliding off the paved area.

EN ROUTE

Once airborne, the degree of necessary vigilance depends largely on the prevailing weather. If the visibility is good and the temperature is below freezing, there is nothing much to worry about. Just listen to the hourly sequence reports to be alerted early of any sudden change in conditions along the route.

Aside from staying clear of the clouds, know the types of precipitation forecast for your route. Dry powder snow, like rain, while reducing forward visibility, represents no particular problem. Freezing rain or wet snow, on the other hand, will adhere to the aircraft and windscreen, reducing forward visibility. Sometimes, when heavy, it will cover the windscreen completely to a degree beyond the capability of the defroster to deal with.

Always continue to keep track of conditions at the destination airport. Remember, when braking action is being reported as medium or poor by a car or truck, it is likely to be worse for an airplane touching down at much higher speeds. In that case, are the runways long enough to permit a safe rollout without using brakes?

LANDING

The thing to worry about is the condition of the runway. If it's dry and clean, fine. If it's slippery, partially or wholly frozen over, or covered with a thin film of snow, land short and slow and don't attempt to use the brakes until much of the speed has been dissipated. If, in addition, there is a crosswind, land on the upwind side of the runway and be prepared to slide sideways once the airplane starts to slow down.

If several inches of snow cover the runway—especially if it is damp snow—keep the nose up and come as close as possible to making a full-stall landing. The sudden braking action as the wheels plow through the snow could put more strain on the nose gear than it is designed to take.

Watch for snow piled high by the sides of the runways and taxiways. These piles tend to get rock-hard and, especially with low-wing aircraft, can lead to dented wingtips.

MAINTENANCE

In addition to normal maintenance, check the following before every flight:

- Are the landing gear struts properly inflated?
- Are there leaks in heater hoses?
- Is the oil in the aircraft of the right weight for the temperature conditions in which you will be operating?

If, of course, you expect to be shuttling between New York and Florida or Idaho and southern California, you might just have to suffer the delays and expense involved with preheating the engine because using too light an oil in warm weather is more harmful than using too heavy an oil in cold weather.

To the knowledgeable pilot willing to take reasonable precautions, winter flying in a light aircraft can be as safe and enjoyable as any other time of year. When the weather is clear, flying over the snow-covered expanse of the Plains States or the intimidating white peaks of the Rockies can be breathtakingly beautiful.

11
Instruments

THERE ARE ONLY TWO WAYS FOR A PILOT TO FIND HIS WAY FROM POINT A TO point B: visually or by reference to navigational aids. In the days before modern electronic aids were a way of life, pilots found their way about (or not) with natural navigational aids, such as rivers, roads, and railways (the latter of which was often referred to as the "Iron Compass").

As the practitioners of aviation became more sophisticated with navigational aids, the skill of *pilotage*, or flight using landmarks, became less important. But good VFR pilots fly with a combination of the old and new skills.

FLIGHT INSTRUMENTS

Throughout much of this book, a great deal of emphasis is placed on the need to control the aircraft by reference to instruments alone. The reason is simple. More often than not, when a VFR pilot gets himself into a marginal-weather situation, he will sooner or later find that he has lost visual contact with outside reference points, forcing him to rely on his instruments in order to return to VFR conditions (FIG. 11-1).

Not too many years ago the training involved in obtaining a private license included no instrument training at all. In those days, flying by reference to instruments was actually considered a common student error. The student was taught to control the

Fig. 11-1. *Once all visual contact with outside reference points is lost, the pilot must learn to ignore seat-of-the-pants sensations and rely solely on instruments.*

aircraft attitude by reference to the horizon, and instructors often covered the instruments in order to force the student to use whatever outside reference was available. He was taught "contact flying"—to respond to what he saw, heard, and felt in "the seat of the pants." Although that technique might have instilled certain skills in some students, we have come to realize that some "seats" were less sensitive than others, and that outside references could not be always guaranteed.

Basic flight training now includes a certain amount of instrument work under the hood. However, whether or not those few exercises are sufficient to last a pilot through years of VFR flying is questionable.

The trouble is that the difference between contact flying and instrument flying is largely psychological. While in contact flying the feel of the airplane is a vital source of information to which the pilot reacts more or less automatically, in instrument flying he must, above all, learn to ignore that feeling because it is based on faulty reactions of the senses to given flight situations.

The human body is simply not designed for flying. Its sensory system is programmed to operate on the ground, reacting to fixed reference points. It is difficult to adjust the habits practiced since early childhood with reference to movement on the ground to the new habits required for instrument flight without recognizing the reasons why the old habits must be consciously ignored.

The primary sensory system that tends to give us trouble is the eustachian tube in the inner ear, which controls our sense of balance. Once deprived of constant correction supplied by visual cues, this sense of balance turns into the equivalent of a used-car salesman in South L.A.—it tells you what it thinks you want to be told, not what is actually fact. Thus, once you are in a bank for even a very brief period of time, your inner ear adjusts to that condition and tries to persuade you that the bank is, in fact, straight and level flight. If you then pay attention to that sensation and want to keep on turning, you will automatically increase the angle of bank, only to be told again, after a moment, that you are flying level. Unless he corrects by reacting to what the instruments show, you will soon find yourself in a screaming spiral.

On the other hand, when you level off after having been in a bank for a few moments, your inner ear will try to convince you at first that you are, in fact, banking in the opposite direction. It's the same feeling you got when you were a child and either rode the merry-go-round too long or stood in place and turned around and around until you were dizzy. Your inner ear had adjusted to the turning so you could keep your balance—until the turning stopped. Then you found that you had not enough balance to walk, or sometimes even stand. Your inner ear was trying to convince you that you were still making revolutions.

Only the instruments are able to provide you with a true picture of the attitude of an aircraft, and the instruments used for this purpose are referred to as *air-data instruments*. They are the altimeter, airspeed indicator, vertical speed indicator, turn-and-bank indicator, and artificial horizon, plus, of course, the magnetic compass and directional gyro. Using these instruments as sources of reliable and accurate information on which to base your control of the aircraft requires that you have a least a smattering of how they work.

Altimeter

The altimeter (FIG. 11-2) reacts to changes in atmospheric pressure. Its reading is only correct when it has been set to the prevailing atmospheric pressure at the location at which the aircraft is being operated. If you have set the altimeter to the atmospheric pressure at your departure airport, which at the time you left was located in a high-

Fig. 11-2. *Altimeter.*

Mitchell Aircraft Instruments, Inc.

pressure area, and read, say, 30.26, and you have since flown into a low-pressure area where a barometer on the ground would read something like 28.87, the altimeter in the aircraft will be reading high, meaning that it will tell you that you are considerably higher than you actually are.

This might not be particularly important when you know that you are several thousand feet above the highest obstacle anywhere in the vicinity, but it can become crucial at low altitudes. It is, therefore, of great importance—especially if you are operating in marginal weather conditions, which, more often than not, are associated with low atmospheric pressure—that you check with the FSS in your area of flight to ascertain the correct local altimeter setting.

Airspeed Indicator

The airspeed indicator (FIG. 11-3) reacts to air pressure in the pitot tube. Its reading is referred to as *indicated airspeed* (IAS) and differs from true airspeed because the thinner air at altitude produces less pitot pressure than does the heavier air near sea level.

Since the primary purpose of flying for most people is to get from one place to the other quickly, we like to convert the IAS reading to TAS because it is always the higher figure, thus making us feel that we are moving with greater speed.

Many modern airspeed indicators have a rotating dial that can be set to read the TAS at any given altitude. Failing that, the TAS can easily be figured by using the E6B computer or a pocket calculator.

Fig. 11-3. *An airspeed indicator with provision to show true airspeed based on altitude and outside air temperature.*

Mitchell Aircraft Instruments, Inc.

In practice, though few of us might be willing to admit it, TAS is really of little importance. It is useless in determining the actual ground speed unless you happen to know the head- or tailwind component at your altitude and position. Neither can it be used in determining how far above stall speed you happen to be operating. The stall speed of an aircraft is given in IAS, not TAS, and it changes neither with altitude nor with temperature and the resulting density altitude (although it is affected by aircraft weight and possible deformation of airfoils resulting from icing or such). This is important to remember because marginal weather conditions frequently cause you to want to climb rapidly or make steep turns, either of which can cause you to inadvertently get dangerously close to a stall. About the only genuine value for TAS is as an analytical base to compare one airplane model with another.

When you are deprived of visual reference to outside cues, the airspeed indicator is an important instrument in keeping you posted as to the attitude of the aircraft. When the nose is raised above the horizontal plane, airspeed will drop. When the nose is lowered, airspeed will rise. This is especially important during slow flight—or flight at extremely high altitudes—when you tend to be operating at an excessively high angle of attack while actually remaining in level flight.

In the event of a failure or malfunction of the suction system that operates the artificial horizon and gyro compass, the airspeed indicator is the only remaining instrument that can help you judge flight attitude, unless the aircraft is equipped with an angle-of-attack indicator, an extremely useful but little-appreciated instrument.

Vertical Speed Indicator

The vertical speed indicator (VSI) tells you the vertical speed in feet per minute at which the aircraft is either climbing or descending. It is useful during prolonged climbs and descents, but its indications tend to lag somewhat and, therefore, are not reliable immediately after a climb or descent has been initiated. It is helpful when you want to trim the airplane for a change in flight altitude at a specific rate, but is best thought of as a secondary instrument.

Turn-and-Bank Indicator

The turn-and-bank, or needle-and-ball (FIG. 11-4), indicator is useful primarily in helping you to make coordinated turns and preventing you from slipping or skidding. It can also be helpful in setting up a continuous-rate turn, although most pilots prefer to use the artificial horizon for this purpose.

Artificial Horizon

The artificial horizon is, without a doubt, the primary instrument used when controlling the aircraft by reference to instruments alone. It displays the position of the wings with reference to the horizon, is calibrated to show the degree of any bank, and

Fig. 11-4. *Turn-and-bank indicator.*

displays the position of the nose of the aircraft in reference to level. In its display, the aircraft symbol is fixed while the horizon line moves.

Initially, students are psychologically conditioned to think of the horizon as a fixed line and the aircraft as something that moves with reference to that fixed horizon, and often find it difficult to interpret the readings quickly. However, a bit of training and experience quickly teaches them to read this instrument instantaneously.

Although it is possible (and a part of actual instrument training) to control the attitude of the airplane by needle-and-ball and airspeed alone, it is considerably more difficult, and the untrained VFR pilot should be warned against taking a chance of getting into instrument conditions in an aircraft that is not equipped with a working artificial horizon.

Magnetic Compass

The magnetic compass (FIG. 11-5) and the directional gyro are two instruments that must be used in combination. The directional gyro is the primary instrument in maintaining a given heading or turning to a specific heading. However, all directional gyros will gradually *precess*, creeping in one direction or another, and they must, from time to time, be compared with the magnetic compass to make sure that their indication is correct. This comparison must be accomplished while in straight and level flight, since even slight turns, climbs, or descents will cause the magnetic compass to produce an inaccurate reading.

Fig. 11-5. *Magnetic compass.*

INSTRUMENT USE

The VFR pilot without adequate instrument training should make a conscious effort to relax when entering instrument conditions. Excessive tension will lead to overcontrol, which can easily result in what is commonly referred to as *unusual attitudes*.

Banks

Probably the best advice is to take your hands off the control yoke altogether and keep the aircraft straight with just a bit of rudder pressure whenever the instruments show that it is starting into a shallow bank and to keep it in level vertical flight by using the trim wheel. In this manner the aircraft, operating at normal cruise speed, can be kept in level flight and in a wings-level attitude indefinitely (or at least as long as there is fuel in the tanks). Somehow we are less likely to use excessive pressure on the rudder pedals than when we try to correct the flight attitude with our hands on the yoke.

The other advantage is that even if too much pressure is exerted on the rudder pedals, the reaction of the airplane tends to be quite minor, and it is pretty nearly impossible to put the airplane into an unusual attitude through use of the rudder alone.

Unless there is a special reason, such as proximity to the ground or some obstacle, the pilot will probably be better off by spending a few minutes with his hands on his lap, flying the aircraft with just rudder and trim while getting mentally adjusted to the fact that he will have to rely solely upon his instruments in order to eventually get back to VFR conditions.

Turns

There can be no hard and fast rules for the next step. It depends entirely on the conditions that exist and how aware the pilot is of the weather conditions in all directions within range. If you have good reason to believe that, by staying on course at your current altitude, you will soon break out of the clouds, continue on just using your feet, and simply relax and wait. If a turn to the right or left or a complete 180 is indicated, then you eventually will have to use your hands because it would be fairly difficult to try to accomplish a major change in flight direction by rudder alone.

Pay no attention to anything outside the airplane. Keep your eyes on the artificial horizon and don't grab the yoke with clenched fists, but just touch it lightly with the tips of your fingers. Turn just a little at a time and watch the position of the fixed aircraft symbol with reference to the moving horizon. Keep the dot firmly placed on the horizon line and place the wing symbols on a one- or two-dot bank, but no more.

As soon as the desired bank has been established, you might have to neutralize the ailerons in order to prevent the bank from increasing. Depending on the direction of the bank, it might even require opposite aileron to maintain the desired angle.

The aircraft probably will have a tendency to drop its nose slightly, and it will require a light amount of back pressure to keep the dot on the horizon line. Don't overcontrol; very light control inputs are all that are called for.

Once you have established the bank, glance over at the directional gyro (which you should have checked against the magnetic compass before you started the turn) to see how much longer you'll have to stay in the turn until you reach the desired heading. Remember that even though your instruments tell you that you're in a bank, your sense of balance—the inner ear—will try to convince you that you're straight and level. Ignore it!

As soon as you reach the new heading, use a slight amount of aileron pressure to return the wings to a level attitude, and then continue on the new heading using just your feet and the trim wheel as before.

Climbs and Descents

Climbs and descents are best accomplished by strictly keeping your hands off the yoke and using the trim wheel and throttle. At low altitudes, where normal cruise speed is attained at less than full throttle, simply advancing the throttle might accomplish an adequate rate of climb without the need to adjust the trim. At higher altitudes, where full throttle is normally used for cruise, only the trim will need to be adjusted. In aircraft with constant-speed props, don't fool with the rpm. Except in extreme circumstances, the additional climb capability that can be obtained by increasing the rpm is too minimal to worry about.

Descents at any altitude usually can best be set up by simply reducing the throttle setting a fraction, and without bothering with trim. Remember: the less you fool with the controls, the less the chance of getting into trouble because of overcontrol or faulty control application.

If at all possible, try to avoid climbing or descending turns. If both a climb or descent and a turn are indicated, do one at a time. In the case of a climb and turn, climb first to put all possible altitude between you and the ground, and then, once level at the higher altitude, start the turn. In the case of a descent and turn, make the turn first while there is still a lot of room between the airplane and the ground. Then, when the new heading has been established, start the descent.

Practice

All this can, of course, be practiced under a hood in VFR conditions, but not when you're alone in the airplane. Someone should be in the right seat—preferably, though not necessarily, another pilot. He will have to look out for traffic while you are busy keeping your head in the cockpit.

If it's another pilot, he'll know what to do. If it's a nonpilot friend, point out to him where to look for traffic. There's no point in his getting upset about another airplane way above or below. Instruct him carefully in what to look for and where (if traffic is just above the horizon, it is near your altitude; higher than that means it's above you; below the horizon, it is below you), and then sneak a look yourself from time to time, just to make sure that he's doing his job.

Do such practicing at a safe altitude, preferably 5,000 agl or higher and away from heavily traveled airways or busy student training areas. But do practice. It might someday save your life.

12
Navigation Instruments

THE WILLINGNESS OF THE VFR PILOT TO FLY ON TOP OF AN OVERCAST, AT night, or under any other conditions that preclude visual contact with ground-based landmarks should be tempered by his ability to use his navigational equipment with precision. Just because every licensed pilot has once upon a time been taught how to use his VOR and maybe even ADF equipment does not necessarily imply that he'll be able to locate himself precisely over a specific point on the ground if that point is hidden from view. Virtually all of us can recall incidents when we knew perfectly well that we were close to a certain airport where the conditions were 1,500 or 2,000 feet scattered or broken with 3 miles visibility in haze, and we had one heck of a time finding it.

Let's go through a quick refresher course on the use of the various kinds of navigational equipment available in the average better-equipped aircraft today. What we'll be discussing is the basic VHF navigation receiver and the different faces of the associated OBIs, DMEs, ADFs with fixed and rotatable compass roses, simple area navigational equipment, HSIs, Loran, and even wing levelers and autopilots.

VHF NAV RECEIVERS AND OBIs

The purpose of the VHF nav receiver (FIG. 12-1) is to receive signals from VORs and to translate these signals into a cockpit display that, when correctly interpreted by

Fig. 12-1. *Nav receiver (bottom) and OBI (top).*

the pilot, shows the direction of the aircraft's present position from the VOR. This cockpit display, generally known as the Omni Bearing Indicator (OBI), is not affected by the aircraft's direction of flight from one station (FIG. 12-2).

In order to use this equipment to determine the distance from the station, as well as the direction, it is easiest to tune in two VORs and determine the exact position by triangulation. Although triangulation can be done with one receiver and one OBI, by switching back and forth between the frequencies for two stations, it is a lot simpler if two receivers and two OBIs are available (FIG. 12-3). Since an airplane cannot stand still in the air, the time lapse associated with switching from one frequency to another and then readjusting the OBI will materially degrade the precision with which you can determine your position.

An alternate method of determining how far you are from the station—the only available method when only one station is within reception distance—is to fly at right angles to a given radial and watch how long it takes to cross radials that are 10 degrees apart. The formula for this procedure looks like this:

- Time in seconds between bearings (radials) divided by the number of degrees of bearing (radials) change equals minutes to the VOR.

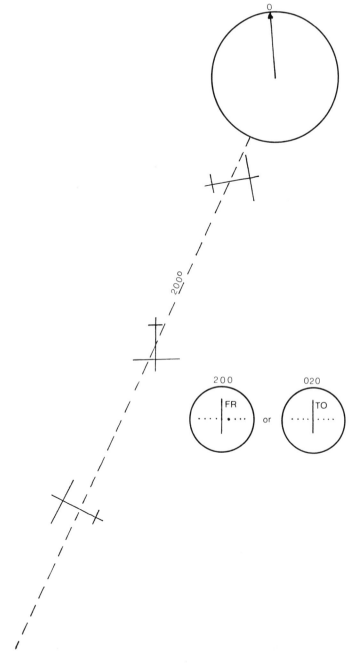

Fig. 12-2. *The OBI shows the radial, or bearing, on which the aircraft is located. It is not affected by the distance from the station or the direction of flight.*

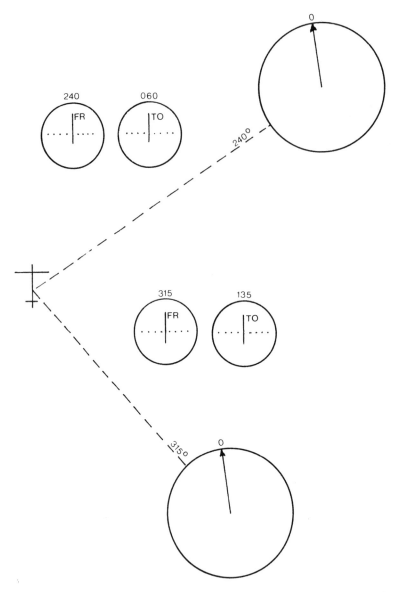

Fig. 12-3. *The exact position of an aircraft can be determined by the process of triangulation, using two VORs.*

- True airspeed (or ground speed, if known) times the minutes between bearings (radials), divided by the degrees of bearing (radial) change equals miles to the station.

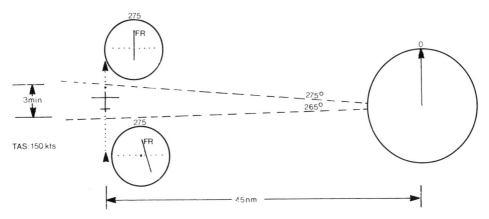

Fig. 12-4. *If it takes an aircraft flying at 150 knots three minutes to cross 10 degrees of radials, the distance to the station is: 150 × 3/.10 = 45 nautical miles.*

If it takes the aircraft 3 minutes to fly a 10-degree bearing change, for example, the aircraft is 18 minutes from the station, assuming that the ground speed remains unchanged:

$$180 \text{ seconds} \div 10 \text{ degrees} = 18 \text{ minutes}$$

Using the second method, if the aircraft is flying at 150 kts (or mph), then the distance to the station is 45 nm (or sm) from the station (FIG. 12-4):

$$\frac{150 \text{ kts} \times 3 \text{ min.}}{10 \text{ degrees}} = 45 \text{ nm}$$

This method of determining position relative to a station is cumbersome and, unless ground speed is known with any degree of precision, it is inexact, but it's better than nothing. Since most of us are unlikely to be able to remember the formulas involved, it might be a good idea to put it on a card and keep it with the charts or in the map compartment.

So far, I have used the faces of conventional OBIs in the illustrations. In recent years, several companies have manufactured OBIs with different displays. Instead of swinging a needle, some use a vertical bar as the course-deviation indicator (CDI). This bar moves from side to side and is somewhat easier to interpret with precision than the swinging needle (FIG. 12-5).

Another company has done away with both the needle and the bar, substituting short vertical electronic bars lined up horizontally. The number of such bars lit indicates the degree of deviation from the selected VOR radial (FIG. 12-6). In addition, several manufacturers, following the trend established by Collins in its Micro Line, have added a radial and bearing readout capability to the nav receiver itself. With this display in the cockpit, you can know at all times the exact radial from or bearing to the

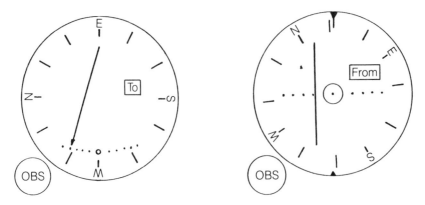

Fig. 12-5. *Two faces of an OBI: one with a swinging needle, one with a moving vertical bar.*

Fig. 12-6. *The face of the OBI developed by Bendix Avionics for its 2000-series navigation instrumentation.*

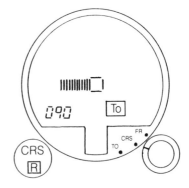

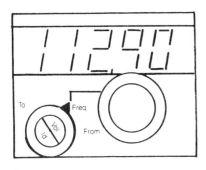

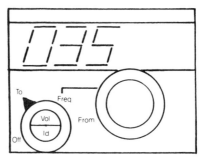

Fig. 12-7. *Additional information displayed by Collins's Micro Line navigation receiver.*

station on which the airplane is located (FIG. 12-7). Having this information constantly available greatly simplifies the task of navigating with precision.

In order to avoid confusion about the different designations and abbreviations used in conjunction with OBIs, FIG. 12-8 shows what is meant by them.

Although few VFR pilots are ever confronted with the need to use localizer frequencies, note that the conventional nav receiver and all OBIs are designed to receive and display not only information relative to VORs, but also to localizers. A *localizer* is a directional beam used by IFR pilots in making instrument approaches to airports equipped with a full ILS or a localizer. They are designed to provide horizontal guidance to the runway, and their frequencies range from 108.1 to 111.9 MHz, all of them using the odd-tenths frequencies only (108.1, 108.3, 108.5, etc.).

When the receiver is tuned to a localizer frequency, the OBS is inoperative and the CDI will react when the aircraft passes anywhere through the area covered by the localizer. When the aircraft is on the localizer centerline, the CDI will be centered; when it is to either side of the centerline, the CDI will be off-center in the direction to which the aircraft must be flown in order to be centered (FIG. 12-9).

Under ordinary circumstances, the ability to receive localizers is of little use in navigation, but occasionally it can be helpful in finding an airport. Since localizer frequencies are not listed on the average aviation charts, the pilot probably would have to call the tower or nearest FSS for that information or refer to the Airport/Facility Directory.

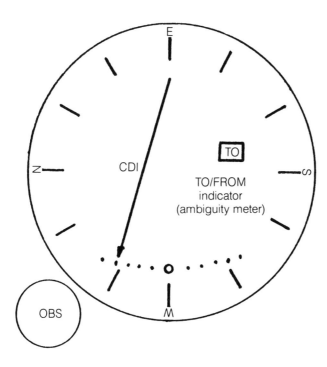

Fig. 12-8. *The various components of an omni-bearing indicator.*

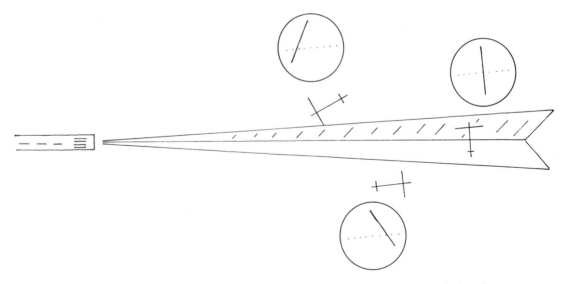

Fig. 12-9. *Indications of the OBI when crossing or flying in the reception area of a localizer.*

DMEs

Distance Measuring Equipment (DME) is marvelously helpful in adding a considerable degree of precision to navigation chores, but because it is quite expensive, it is not often found in lighter and less-equipped aircraft. DME (FIG. 12-10) is so-called pulse equipment because, similar to radar, it transmits pulsed signals to a ground station, which are then returned to the aircraft. By measuring the time it takes for each pulse to make the round trip, the system is capable of figuring out how far from the station the aircraft is located. Then, by measuring the rapidity with which this distance changes when the aircraft is flying either directly to or from such a station, it can figure out the ground speed of the aircraft.

Most DMEs are designed to display either distance to or from the station in nautical miles, ground speed in knots, or the time in minutes, assuming no change in the current ground speed. Some will display only one of these parameters at a time, while others are designed to display several or all these data simultaneously.

The obvious advantage of having DME is that only one station needs to be within reception distance to determine the exact present position. And this information is constantly available to the pilot without the need of bothering with cumbersome triangulations. In addition, by providing ground speed information on a continuous basis, the DME can enable the pilot to compare that information with the TAS and know precisely what wind component is present at his altitude and location. Having this information in front of you simplifies the task of selecting an altitude at which you can take advantage of the greatest tailwind, or conversely, find the flight level with the least headwind.

Fig. 12-10. *A combined VOR, ILS, DME, and marker beacon display unit with DME (digital numbers) in the range mode.*

Narco Avionics, Inc.

However, DMEs only function in conjunction with so-called colocated VOR/DME facilities or with VORTACs; they cannot provide the information referenced to a simple VOR. As a result, the number of stations available for navigation is reduced, but there are adequate numbers of VOR/DMEs and VORTACs in most areas of the country to ensure reception as long as the aircraft is at a reasonable altitude. Figure 12-11 shows the symbols used on aviation charts to differentiate between simple VORs, VOR/DMEs, and VORTACs.

ADFs

The Automatic Direction Finder (ADF) is probably the oldest kind of electronic navigation equipment, and although today it is relegated to a position of secondary importance, it still comes in handy (FIG. 12-12). While VOR receivers are designed to tell you the location of the aircraft relative to the station regardless of direction of flight, the ADF display shows you the direction to the station relative to the nose of the aircraft.

There are two basic types of ADF displays. One has a fixed compass card on which zero always coincides with the nose of the fixed aircraft symbol. The other has a compass rose, which can be rotated by the pilot to place the heading at which he is currently flying under the nose of the fixed aircraft symbol. The latter is a lot easier to use because it relieves the pilot of the chore of mentally figuring out what the needle

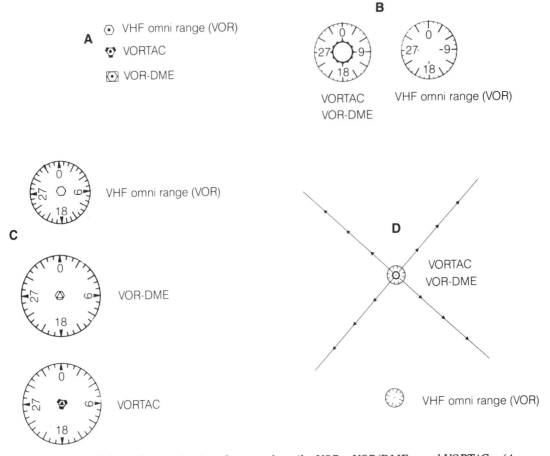

Fig. 12-11. *Symbols used on navigation charts to describe VORs, VOR/DMEs, and VORTACs. (A = sectional and WAC charts; B = Jeppesen low-altitude en route charts; C = NOAA low-altitude en route charts; D = Jeppesen area navigation en route charts.)*

deflection means in terms of actual direction from the aircraft to the station (FIG. 12-13).

Most of the time the average VFR pilot will use his ADF to fly to a station and to know when he crosses over that station. He will not, and probably should not, attempt to use it to navigate away from a station, since this procedure requires considerable practice.

ADFs operate on frequencies between 190 and 1799.95 kHz, which include Non-Directional Beacons (NDBs), compass locators (LOMs), and standard AM broadcast stations. When tuned to any of these facilities, the needle will point toward the transmitting station, and the pilot can navigate toward that station simply by keeping the needle right under the nose of the fixed airplane symbol.

Fig. 12-12. *A digital ADF tuner with display head and rotatable azimuth card.*

However, the frequencies in this range are affected by nearly everything: rain, sleet, snow, thunderstorms, mountains, coastlines, disturbances in the upper atmosphere, day, night, dusk, and dawn. The farther from the station you are and the higher the frequency, the more serious the errors are likely to be. During daylight hours, when the weather is halfway decent (and when none of the aforementioned exceptions are present), ADF reception is usually quite reliable. At dusk and dawn, however, it is notoriously unreliable, and it is less reliable at night than during the day. In addition, even though the frequency allocations for NDBs and standard broadcast stations are made to theoretically avoid interference with one another, there are times when signals can "skip" like a flat rock on the water and jam signals of stations located incredible distances apart. (Once, while flying at night from Phoenix to Los Angeles, I found myself listening to perfectly clear reception from a broadcast station that turned out to be in Philadelphia.)

It is important, therefore, to always make certain that the station being used is, in fact, the station you think it is. This is easy with NDBs and other low-frequency nav aids, which broadcast an oral identification signal. It is more complicated in the case of standard broadcast stations, which often identify themselves only once every half

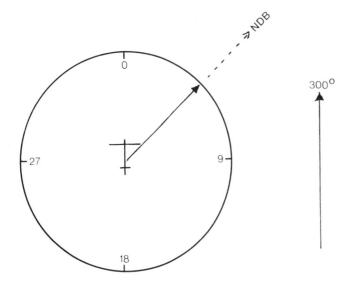

Fig. 12-13. *The difference in the ADF display between units with stationary and rotatable compass roses.*

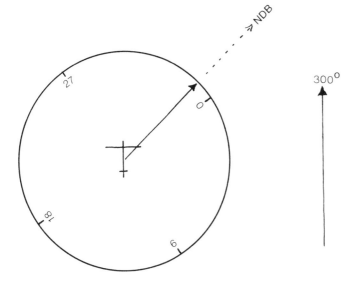

hour or so, and then not necessarily exactly on the hour or half hour.

It is important to know if the needle of the particular ADF installed in the airplane has a regular *park position*, a position to which it moves when no adequate signal is being received. It could simply stop moving, thus giving no visual indication that it is no longer pointing to any particular station. Unless the station-identification code is being monitored, flying according to the ADF needle could result in drastic navigational errors.

The sound is usually a tip-off. If it is filled with static and cuts out intermittently, it is safe to assume that the signal is unreliable regardless of what the needle does. Conversely, if the sound comes in strong and steady without obvious interferences (even though the sound of most ADFs is pretty bad), it can be assumed that the needle indication is reliable.

With an ADF needle always pointing to the station, and if that station is your destination or checkpoint, the logical assumption would be to align the needle with the nose of the airplane and then to keep it there until the needle flips 180 degrees, which would indicate station passage. This method works fine if there is no crosswind. If there is, you would have to fly a curved track which, if the crosswind is of considerable velocity, might add quite a few miles to the distance being covered. In that situation the thing to do is to fly a heading and apply the necessary crosswind correction (the slower the aircraft, the more the correction), using the ADF needle as a backup, rather than as the primary navigational aid.

As long as you fly to the station, things are fairly simple. But they get a bit muddled when you fly from the station. The needle will point straight to the tail of the airplane no matter what direction you fly from the station. In this case, you must fly a heading, using the needle to keep track of whether a crosswind is causing you to drift off course. When this happens, the needle will begin to point several degrees to one side or the other of the tail. You then need to make a course correction in the direction of the needle. You should continue that turn until the needle indicates twice the number of degrees as before. Continue on that heading until the needle shows the same deviation as was shown before you started the correction. Then turn back on course, keeping the needle a few degrees off the tail in the direction from which the wind is blowing (FIG. 12-14).

In the United States, where there is no shortage of VORs, the ADF is usually considered a secondary instrument, except in the case of instrument pilots, who use it in making ADF approaches. But once you go beyond the borders of this country, you will find that VORs are few and far between, and there the ADF becomes your only means of navigating.

AREA NAVIGATION EQUIPMENT

Unless or until they have had an opportunity to fly with it, some VFR pilots will consider Area Navigation equipment (RNAV) as an aid for lazy pilots—an expensive frill that cannot replace good old-fashioned navigational skills and a system that does little to enhance the ease and safety of VFR flight. Nothing could be further from the truth. The capabilities of RNAV, when fully and correctly understood and used will greatly enhance the ability of the VFR pilot to cope with the many weather and navigational problems that he is likely to encounter.

RNAV, in principle, provides the pilot with the ability to electronically relocate VOR/DME or VORTAC stations to any position within 100 to 150 nm of its actual location. To accomplish this, the system utilizes the capabilities of an all-purpose digi-

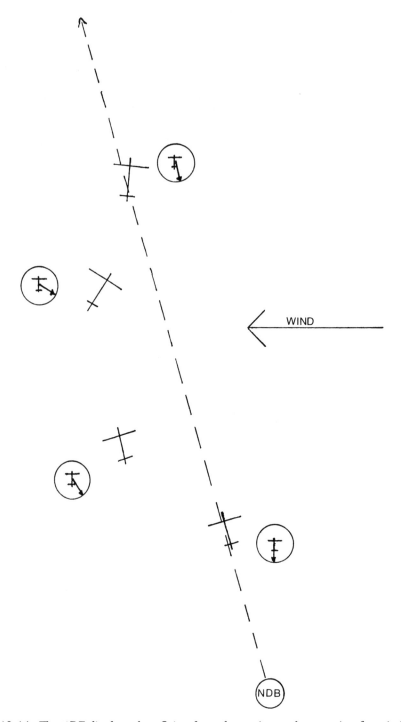

Fig. 12-14. *The ADF display when flying from the station and correcting for wind drift.*

Fig. 12-15. *A typical area navigation (RNAV) system.*

tal computer in conjunction with a conventional nav receiver, OBI, and DME. Both
the nav receiver and the DME are tuned to the same VORTAC. The computer is then
told at what distance and on what radial from the station the pilot wants to establish a
"phantom" VOR, which is referred to as a *waypoint* (W/P).

The interface between the pilot and the computer is the so-called *control-display
unit*, or CDU (FIG. 12-15). It is equipped with push buttons or concentric knobs to
enter digital data into the computer, plus a display window, which shows the pilot the
coordinates of the waypoint in question.

When the RNAV system is activated and a waypoint selected, the CDI needle in
the OBI operates in relation to that waypoint just as if it were an actual VOR, the only
difference being that the needle deflection is *linear*, meaning that a deflection of a
given number of dots always indicates a given number of nautical miles off course,
rather than a given number of degrees (FIG. 12-16). Also, the DME will display nautical miles to the waypoint, ground speed, or time to the waypoint at the current ground
speed.

Finding the Airport with RNAV

One of the most obvious and basic examples of using RNAV is in the context of
finding an airport that has no nav aid associated with it. The pilot checks his charts for
the radial from a nearby VORTAC on which that airport is located and measures the
distance along that radial. He then feeds that information into the RNAV computer
and, presto, there is a VOR in the form of a waypoint right on top of the airport. Then,
even if the visibility is reduced by haze, smoke, smog, or whatever, he simply flies to
that waypoint, knowing that when he gets there he is exactly over the airport (FIG.
12-17).

RNAV and Marginal Weather

Let's take a look at that familiar VFR situation in which you want to take a look
into marginal weather conditions to see if you can go on, or if farther on it's getting so
bad that you might have to turn back.

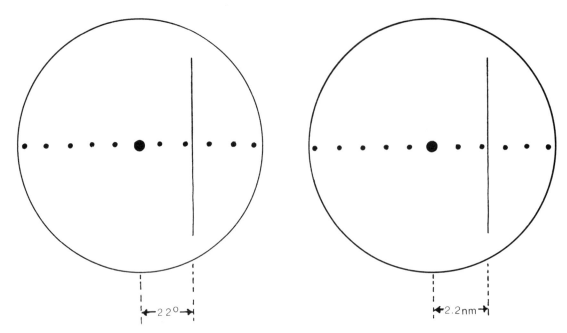

Fig. 12-16. *In the VOR mode, the CDI is angular, showing degrees off the radial (left). In the RNAV mode it is linear, showing nautical miles off the radial (right).*

Pick a VORTAC located some distance ahead—30 to 40 nm—along your desired route. Use it to establish a waypoint over an airport that is located in the clear somewhere near the point where the weather begins to get bad. Now you can fly into the marginal conditions and, if you choose, continue on your course for as far as you can receive the VORTAC to which your waypoint is referenced. Depending on your level of flight, in this instance it would mean that you can go on for some 80 nm without losing the waypoint. If you then find that you simply can't go on, you can navigate back to the airport on which you have placed the waypoint, find it without difficulty, and land (FIG. 12-18).

Or, let's assume that the winds aloft are such that it is important for you to know constantly how long it will take you to get to your destination, which might be 200 nm away. This situation is a little trickier. You select a number of VORTACs more or less along your intended flight path and establish a number of waypoints all at the same location—namely your destination. By doing so, you will get a constant DME readout with reference to your destination telling you, for instance, whether or not you have sufficient fuel to get there with the prevailing headwind component (FIG. 12-19).

The potential uses of RNAV are so varied that it would be impossible to describe all of them in these pages. Suffice it to say that RNAV greatly enhances the ability of the VFR (and IFR) pilot to navigate with precision, regardless of whether he is flying along established airways or on a direct route along a course that is not defined by

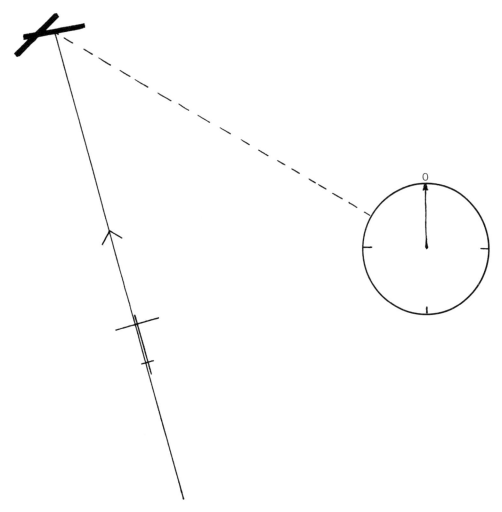

Fig. 12-17. *By inserting the radial and distance from the station at which the airport is located into the RNAV computer, you can place a waypoint right on top of the airport.*

ground-based nav aids. It takes a bit of practice, experience, and imagination to use RNAV to its fullest (FIG. 12-20).

HSIs

The Horizontal Situation Indicator (HSI) is, in fact, a more sophisticated version of an OBI (usually also including a glide slope display). The average HSI consists of a directional gyro (usually slaved), a heading bug, a CDI, a TO/FROM indicator, and a stationary aircraft symbol, plus a glide slope indicator (FIG. 12-21).

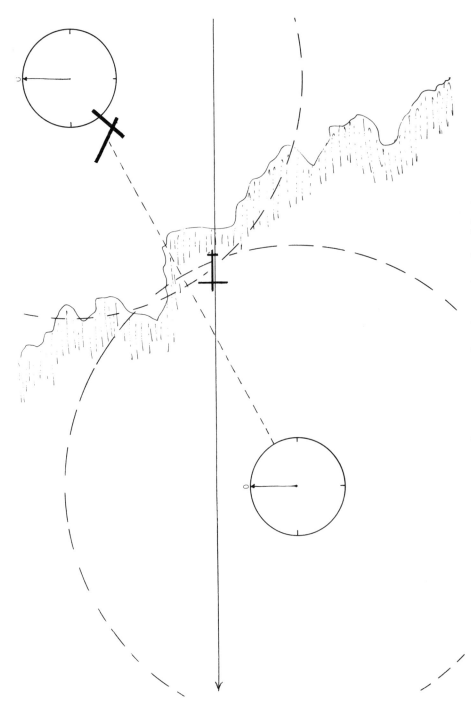

Fig. 12-18. *RNAV can be useful in providing a safe escape route when the weather ahead begins to turn sour.*

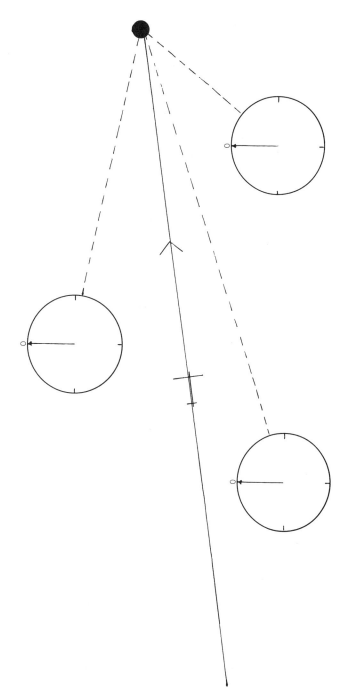

Fig. 12-19. *If you place a series of waypoints over your destination, the DME will always read distance and time to the destination.*

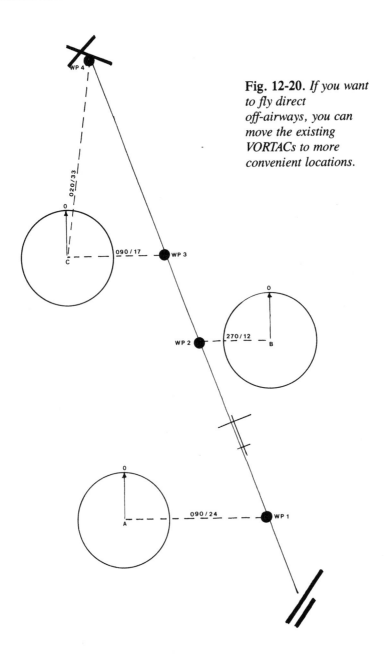

Fig. 12-20. *If you want to fly direct off-airways, you can move the existing VORTACs to more convenient locations.*

The DG is just like any such vacuum instrument with a rotating compass rose that, when related to the stationary aircraft symbol in the center, indicates in which direction the nose of the aircraft is pointing. The term *slaved* means that the annoying precession problem is corrected automatically by a magnetic azimuth transmitter, also called a *flux detector* or *flux gate*. This instrument is affixed to the aircraft in an area

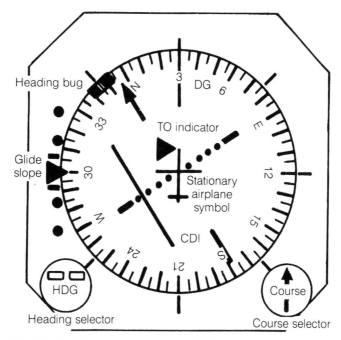

Fig. 12-21. *The components of an HSI.*

free of magnetic disturbances. It senses the alignment of the aircraft with respect to the earth's magnetic field and sends that information to the DG, causing it to constantly align itself with magnetic north.

The heading bug is hand-set by the pilot to remind him of his intended flight path. It can be coupled to an autopilot with heading hold, which will then turn the aircraft automatically to keep the heading bug aligned with its nose (FIG. 12-22).

The CDI performs the same function usually performed by the CDIs in OBIs. The needle shows the aircraft's position relative to a selected VOR radial or bearing, except that this presentation, once understood, is easier and faster to interpret than the CDI in an OBI.

Fig. 12-22. *The heading bug can be set by the pilot and coupled to the autopilot.*

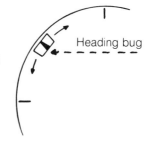

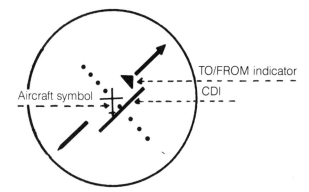

Fig. 12-23. *The CDI is an arrow with a movable center section. In order to get back onto the radial, the pilot flies in the direction in which that center section is displaced (toward the needle).*

The CDI consists of an arrow with a movable center section. By turning the course-selector knob, you can turn it to a desired bearing to or a radial from the station. If, when this is done, the center section moves to the left, it means that the aircraft is to the right of the bearing or radial and must turn left in order to intercept it. If the center section moves to the right, the opposite is true. By relating the fixed aircraft symbol to the movable center section of the arrow, you will always know the appropriate course corrections (FIG. 12-23).

The TO/FROM indicator, also called the *ambiguity meter*, shows whether the selected radial indicates the direction from or to the VOR. It is usually a triangle resembling a stylized arrowhead, rather than a flag reading **TO** or **FROM**.

The aircraft symbol in the center of the HSI is stationary and always points to the twelve o'clock position. When trying to interpret the instrument indications with respect to the aircraft, think of yourself as being above the aircraft, looking down. Figures 12-24 and 12-25 show the various HSI indications during a typical horizontal and vertical maneuver.

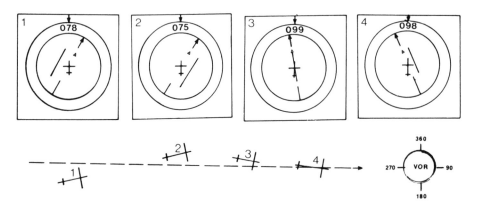

Fig. 12-24. *The HSI indication while a pilot tries to stay on the 270-degree radial (90-degree bearing) from a station, flying in an easterly direction.*

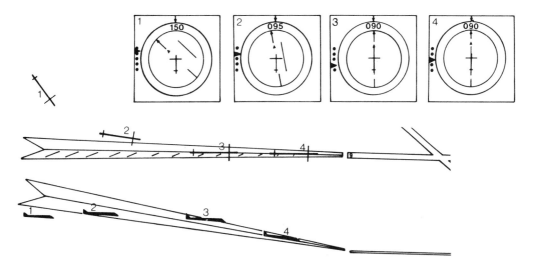

Fig. 12-25. *The HSI indications while intercepting a localizer and glide slope.*

LORAN C

Loran C is probably the most revolutionary navigation aid since the compass. When a pilot enters a longitude/latitude coordinate—for instance a destination airport—the computer displays the heading, distance, and other information. Or ask the computer where you are and it will indicate the airplane's longitude/latitude; no VOR radials, no RNAV computations, and no DME.

Reception is so reliable in most parts of the United States that Loran C is approved for limited IFR use. Also, thanks to electronics miniaturization, a Loran C receiver can be installed in the smallest airplane—even ultralights—or carried aboard as a portable unit.

Since this book deals with flying in poor conditions, rather than this section being "everything you always wanted to know about Loran C," it will be merely an overview.

In his book *Flying with Loran C*, TAB book No. 2370, Bill Givens puts it in perspective: "Loran, (an) acronym for *Lo*ng *Ra*nge *N*avigation, (is) a method of measuring the position of an aircraft or boat by measuring the time difference between two sets of low-frequency radio signals propagated by a Loran chain station." (*Editor's note: Flying with Loran C* is no longer in print. For more information on Loran C, refer to *The Art of Instrument Flying-2nd Edition*, TAB book No. 3654, by J.R. Williams.)

If an airplane is equipped with a functioning Loran C receiver and the pilot knows how to operate it, that pilot should be able to fly to practically any point he desires. If the weather turns sour and visibility drops to IFR conditions while he is en route, a pilot could lay in a course to good weather, fly by referring to the unit, and proceed to his destination in VFR conditions.

It's been a whirlwind romance between Loran C and general aviation. Givens's book says VFR pilots were using Loran C in the late 1970s, and the FAA approved the first helicopter installation in 1979 for IFR operations. The first airplane certification for IFR operation came in 1981 in a state-owned twin-engine Beech. And, as the cliché says, the rest is history.

By the mid-1980s, the Aircraft Electronics Association (AEA) estimated that between 27,000 and 28,000 Loran C units were flying in general aviation airplanes, according to *Business and Commercial Aviation*. The avionics industry believes demand will continue, bolstered by approvals for non-precision-instrument approaches using Loran C and increased efforts to get full coverage in the continental United States, the magazine stated. To get full coverage, a midcontinent "gap" where IFR accuracy is not assured would be eliminated by adding new stations. (VFR operators may legally use Loran C in that "gap.")

Regardless of its intended use, VFR or IFR, Loran C is safety insurance, which could pay for itself in fuel savings with direct flights. Fierce competition in the avionics marketplace, fueled by supply and demand, has driven the price down to reasonable levels. Getting acquainted with Loran C, and possibly acquiring a unit, could prove to be a livesaver in poor weather some day.

WING LEVELERS AND AUTOPILOTS

Ever since Mooney started to furnish a wing leveler as standard equipment on its aircraft some 15 years ago, the number of weather-related accidents involving VFR pilots and Mooneys has dropped noticeably. The fact is that the cause of most of such accidents—beyond the obvious flight into instrument conditions—is the inability of the VFR pilot to maintain control over the aircraft on instruments.

Basically all aircraft, although relatively stable, will eventually start to drop one wing, and this initially shallow bank will gradually increase to steeper and steeper angles unless the pilot uses the controls to correct the situation. Not so if the aircraft is equipped with a wing leveler or autopilot: Even the simplest form of wing leveler will hold the wings steady for an indefinite period of time and will relevel them if the pilot has forced the aircraft into a bank. In addition, all have means of initiating a shallow turn, which maintains a constant shallow bank angle.

With these capabilities on the aircraft, the VFR pilot is relieved of much of the complication associated with controlling the aircraft by reference to the instruments. He can, instead, concentrate on the best way back to VFR conditions, can study his charts, and can communicate with Flight Service Stations on the ground without worrying that the airplane will suddenly do him dirty.

Simple wing levelers are available at reasonable prices for single-engine aircraft. An optional feature that is highly recommended is an *autopilot*, which automatically navigates on a given bearing or radial to or from a VOR. Considering the cost of airplanes and just about everything associated with them, this is about the cheapest insurance a VFR pilot can buy.

The one negative aspect of flying a wing leveler or autopilot-equipped aircraft is the increased temptation to fly into instrument conditions, because much of the danger factor has been eliminated. Always remember that, any time a VFR pilot flies into IFR conditions without communicating with ATC, there is the danger of IFR traffic operating in the area, and the VFR pilot is endangering not only his own life and aircraft, but those of his passengers, as well.

It is unavoidable in a book of this type that we must talk frequently about actions that are not only illegal, but also dangerous to the occupants of the aircraft involved and to other innocent aircraft that are operating quite legally in the same airspace. It can't be emphasized too frequently or too strongly that such illegal operations in instrument conditions should be considered only as a last resort. Any rogue pilot who habitually ignores the FARs and blithely operates on instruments without bothering to obtain an ATC clearance is, in fact, a menace to aviation in general and himself in particular.

13
A Matter of Balance

THE EXPERIENCE YEARS AGO TAUGHT ONE PILOT ABOUT THE IMPORTANCE of one kind of balance when he flew. He was about to embark on a lengthy trip in his Piper Tri-Pacer from Santa Monica, California, to the East Coast. With him were his wife and his son's girlfriend, who was going to meet the pilot's son in Boston where he was in school.

WEIGHT AND BALANCE
Loaded

Not aware of the importance of weight in a light aircraft, the two women showed up with every conceivable piece of luggage, and the pilot himself also brought quite a bit because he was planning on doing business while on the trip.

On the day of the departure, the weather was beautiful—none of the low clouds, fog, and smog that so often plague the Los Angeles Basin. Once at the airport, the pilot made sure that the Piper was fully fueled and then loaded all of the bags into the rear of the cabin. It filled not only the luggage compartment, but was also piled high on half of the rear seat.

The pilot had not yet accumulated a great amount of experience. He had obtained his private license only months before, and after purchasing the second-hand airplane he had made only a few trips in it—and then always solo. His flight training had failed to include lessons on the subject of weight and balance, and it never occurred to him that, with three adults and all that luggage aboard, he might find the airplane would balk at the load.

The first sign that something was amiss occurred when the younger woman was the first to board, climbing into the rear seat while the pilot was still doing his pre-flight check. Suddenly the airplane tipped back, raising the nosewheel off the ground and coming to a rest on its tail!

But the pilot still wasn't alarmed. He figured that as soon as his weight was in the front seat, the situation would automatically rectify itself—and, at least for the moment, he was quite right. As soon as he and his wife settled into the front seats, the plane righted itself and there seemed to be no further problem.

He taxied to the end of the runway. Since it was one of those rare days when an easterly wind was present, he was instructed to use Runway 3. He would be taking off to the east over the city and would be able to continue straight out over Los Angeles and on toward Beaumont Pass.

Cleared for takeoff, he pulled into position, fed in full throttle, and was surprised to find that it seemed to take a lot longer than usual to become airborne. But eventually the stubby little airplane did lift off, and started to climb at a depressingly low rate. Granted, he attained sufficient altitude to clear any obstacles safely, but all he seemed to be able to coax out of the airplane was something less than a 100 fpm climb. In addition, he slowly became aware that, even though the nose was trimmed down, the airplane insisted on flying in a nose-high attitude—mushing, rather than flying the way it had usually done.

By the time they were passing over the eastern portion of L.A., they had only managed 1,600 feet, and although he had never before flown out of the area to the east before, he knew from his charts that they'd have to get up quite a bit in order to clear the various mountains between Los Angeles and Phoenix, their first stop.

He was only then beginning to realize that the problem was not with the airplane, but with all the extra weight. Something had to be done because they couldn't possibly fly all the planned trip with the airplane behaving the way it did.

Time to Unload

Knowing that both his passengers were in a light airplane for the first time, he hated to add to their quite natural apprehensions (as well as his own) by admitting that something was wrong, but there just wasn't any alternative, so he told them that he'd have to go back to Santa Monica and get rid of some of the luggage because the airplane was quite obviously overloaded.

By now, he was actually beginning to worry about keeping the Piper in the air, and he made a very wide and shallow 180 to head back. It worked. They got back to the airport, landed, and to the dismay of his passengers, the pilot unloaded and stored every piece of superfluous luggage in his car, locked it, and then tried the flight again.

This time, the Tri-Pacer behaved the way it should and, only a little over an hour later, they were again on their way to Phoenix, El Paso, and beyond.

Later, after the pilot had accumulated a fair number of hours in the left seat of a variety of airplanes, thinking back on that day made his skin crawl. By now he had become familiar—in theory at least—with the drastic effects that can result from ignoring the weight-and-balance limitations of an airplane. Especially with too much weight concentrated aft of the center of gravity, it is quite possible to experience a situation in which the aircraft can no longer be trimmed for level flight and, despite the best efforts of its pilot, might enter a stall.

On that particular day, it was a lucky break that the air was smooth. If there had been any serious turbulence, it easily could have resulted briefly in an angle of attack too extreme to keep the airplane flying, and a stall with that load condition would, more likely than not, have turned into a spin from which recovery at that altitude would have been impossible.

THE CONCRETE BEHIND— ANOTHER KIND OF BALANCE

It used to be standard procedure for ground control to issue taxi clearances to the end of the active runway unless the pilot requested an intersection takeoff. Now, with

Fig. 13-1. *Requesting the full length of the runway tends to make the pilot feel that he is admitting to a lack of proficiency.*

more and more 2-mile-long jet runways, light aircraft are frequently given taxi clearance to the most convenient intersection even without a request from the pilot.

For all practical purposes, nothing has changed. While it used to be up to the pilot to request the intersection, it is now up to him to request the full length of the runway. The difference is psychological. Requesting an intersection takeoff makes the pilot feel that he is telling the controller he is a good enough pilot to get his aircraft safely airborne in less than the full length of the runway. On the other hand, requesting the full length seems to imply a lack of proficiency, especially when the runway is a long one (FIG. 13-1). As a result, pilots are prone to accept intersection takeoffs even though they might realize that they are taking a calculated risk.

How Much Is Enough?

The question that few light plane pilots are able to answer with certainty is: How much runway is enough? We all know, or at least should know, the minimum field length required to clear a 50-foot obstacle. This figure is listed in the owner's manual.

But do we always remember how the field length was determined? It was in an airplane at full gross weight, with a brand-new engine, flown by an expert test pilot, and the figure is where the aircraft is able to get off in time to clear that theoretical obstacle at a sea-level airport where the runway is smooth, the temperature is 59 °F, and there is no wind.

But what about a more realistic scenario when the temperature is 85 °F, the runway is rough, the field elevation is 4,000 feet, and there is a gusty crosswind? And how much additional runway would you need if the engine suddenly started to act up just as you were about to lift off and you have to shut everything down and try to get stopped before running through the fence at the end of the runway?

Balanced Field Length

Instead of listing minimum field lengths, the performance figures for jet aircraft include so-called *balanced-field-length* numbers, which represent the distance necessary to accelerate to liftoff speed and then come to a full stop. This is a much more meaningful figure, but it is not readily available (nor is it required by the FAA for certification) for light aircraft, although some manufacturers have started including accelerate-stop distance in their published performance parameters. As a general rule, it is safe to assume that the accelerate-stop distance is approximately twice the 50-foot-obstacle-clearance distance—even more if the runway is wet.

This might seem like a lot of talk about nothing. After all, most of us would have a tough time remembering when we last abandoned a takeoff. But that doesn't mean it might not become necessary tomorrow. The reasons for at least considering aborting a takeoff are legion:

- A bug crawls into the pitot tube and there is no airspeed indication
- Just at liftoff a door pops open

- While accelerating, the pilot drops his glasses and they slip behind the rudder pedals
- The door was inadvertently closed on a seat belt, and it's now banging against the fuselage
- An engine malfunction or actual failure occurs

And don't fool yourself into thinking that just because you're flying a twin that you always have the other engine to complete the takeoff, go around, and then land again. Half the light twins flying probably don't have sufficient single-engine climb capability to get the aircraft over the trees past the end of the runway. (It has been said, half-jokingly, that flying a twin-engine aircraft simply means that you will get to the scene of its crash quicker.)

It's something to think about the next time you're cleared for an intersection take-off. How much runway is left and how much do you need to accelerate and then stop—in case one of those bugaboos shows up just as the wheels are about to lift off the concrete.

So the controller thinks you're an old fuddy-duddy because you're asking for twice as much runway as you'll actually be using. So what? Let him think what he wants. It's not his life that might be at stake; it's yours and your passengers'.

Always remember the old cliché: There is nothing more useless than the sky above, the fuel on the ground, and the concrete behind.

14
Grayout

THE PILOT WAS ON HIS WAY FROM THE EAST COAST TO DETROIT. HE HAD flown from New York more or less straight west and had reached the southern shore of Lake Erie somewhere west of the city of Erie and east of Cleveland. Despite a fairly high overcast, the weather had been fine so far, with, for this part of the country, pretty good visibility.

Ever since the lake had come into view, he had been arguing with himself about whether to fly across the lake on the straight route to Detroit or whether to stay over dry land and fly the detour via Cleveland and Toledo. The difference in distance and, therefore, time as well as fuel, would be considerable. From his present position, straight across the water, would involve about 100 nm, while flying around the lake would nearly double that figure.

The weather for Detroit was reported as 3,000-foot overcast, visibility five in smoke and haze. Cleveland was reporting 6,000-foot overcast, visibility four. In other words, if he flew across the water, the overcast would probably be lowering somewhat along the way, but it shouldn't be any serious problem except that, by having to fly about 2,000 feet above the water, he'd be out of sight of land and, of course, out of gliding distance for some time (FIG. 14-1).

Oh, what the heck, the airplane doesn't care whether it's flying over land or water, so why should he? He tuned his OBI to the 286-degree radial from the Jefferson

Fig. 14-1. *Having to fly at about 2,000 feet, he would be out of sight of land and gliding distance for a long time.*

VOR, which should take him past Windsor, Ontario, on the south and straight toward Detroit. And now, keeping the needle centered, he headed out over the water.

EVERYTHING WAS FINE

At first, everything was fine. He was flying at 4,500 feet, and he watched the lake shore gradually disappear behind him. He did wish that he would be able to see the horizon more clearly, but everything in the distance seemed to dissolve into some sort of featureless gray. There was no wind to speak of, and the water below was also calm and without distinctive features, except for a freighter to his left, steaming eastward.

He had been over the water for about 10 minutes when it became obvious that the ceiling was beginning to press down on him, and he dropped to a lower altitude, leveling eventually at 2,000 feet. With the surface of the lake being at around 575 feet, this put him at about 1,400 feet agl. At this lower altitude, he could see whatever wavelets there were below more clearly, but straight ahead and in all directions all he could see was gray water merging into gray haze and gray sky (FIG. 14-2).

He was aware that even though it was certainly technically VFR, he was, in fact, on instruments and wished that he had a wing leveler or autopilot, which didn't need a horizon in order to keep the aircraft straight and level.

Fig. 14-2. *In all directions, all he could see was gray water.*

TIME PASSED SLOWLY

In such a situation, time has a way of passing slower than normal. Time and again he would look at his watch, only to realize that just a minute or two had passed. No matter how hard he tried, there was simply nothing his eye could fasten on except the water below, and even it seemed so calm and flat as to be meaningless (FIG. 14-3).

By now, the overcast was not too far above him, and he wondered what he would do if it forced him down even lower. The trouble was that the overcast was just a solid sheet of gray, and he couldn't even be sure where it was, except that he knew he was not in it. If it did drop down, would he be able to see it before he found himself suddenly in the clouds? After all, with everything around him being just one shade of dirty gray, how would he know if what he was flying into was simply more of the same old haze or actually some lower clouds?

He remembered reading about pilots flying over Greenland and being caught in a *whiteout*—where everything around them was white—and there was at least one story about someone landing in the snow without realizing it.

Well, at least he still had the water to look at, and the OBI—or did he? He suddenly realized that the CDI needle had remained so firmly centered, not because of his faultless navigation, but because it had ceased receiving signals from the VOR. He had simply failed to notice the OFF flag.

Fig. 14-3. *No matter how hard he tried, there was nothing his eyes could fasten on, knowing that if it were clear he would see the shoreline and mountains.*

He tuned the nav receiver to the Windsor VOR, but to no avail. He remembered noticing the minimum transmission altitude for his route to be listed as 2,400 feet on the Jepp chart, and he figured, probably correctly, that he must be somewhere in the middle of the lake where, at his low level of flight, he'd be beyond reception distance for either station.

But, after all, there wasn't much chance of getting lost. Even if he should inadvertently drift off course, he'd have to reach one of the shores sooner or later, and with the water below barely moving, he had to assume that there wasn't enough wind to be of consequence. Well, he'd just have to sit there and be patient and hope that the ceiling wouldn't play any tricks on him.

Again, minutes seemed to be stretching into hours, but eventually there was a shudder in the CDI needle, the OFF flag popped back and forth and then disappeared for good, and the needle settled slightly to the right of center. Apparently, he had done pretty well in terms of holding his heading because he did want to pass Windsor to the south, meaning that the needle would be to the right as long as the OBI was set to his heading, rather than the actual radial from Windsor on which he was at any given moment.

THEN THERE WAS A SHIP

And then there was a ship, and then another, and after a few more minutes he thought he saw some sort of a dark line way ahead in the distance. The shore? He continued to peer into the haze, and the dark line got darker and more distinct. True enough, it was the shore, and finally there was something for him to look at again. He breathed a sigh of relief, surprised that the appearance of an indication of dry land should make him feel so much better.

Actually it all had been perfectly simple. Nothing to it. Whatever there had been that had been bothersome had been his own apprehensions. Granted, if the engine had decided to act up or if there had been some other malfunction, he might have been in some fairly serious trouble.

People were probably right when they said that you shouldn't fly across any of the Great Lakes except on clear days when you can climb to 10,000 or 12,000 feet, thus reducing the time beyond gliding distance to shore to an acceptable minimum. But there was the shore, Canada to the right, the good old United States to the left and straight ahead, and along with it the smoke and air pollution, which is one of the distinguishing characteristics of Detroit.

All he had to do now was to find Detroit City Airport, and he'd be home free.

15
Flying to Air Shows

THERE ISN'T ANYTHING DIFFERENT ABOUT FLYING TO THE LOCATION OF an air show except that, once you get close to your destination, there is often a disproportionately high amount of traffic. Year after year, the number of aircraft movements recorded at major air shows—as well as air races, glider and balloon meets, and similar aviation events—exceed those that are normally handled by some of the busiest hubs in the country (FIG. 15-1). The unprepared pilot attending one of these events for the first time might become unnecessarily intimidated as he listens to the never-ending radio chatter while still 30 or 40 miles from his destination.

ADVANCE PREPARATIONS

As with virtually everything in aviation, a bit of advance preparation will tend to minimize the problems to be faced. Nearly all aviation events that can be expected to attract large numbers of aircraft are associated with some nonstandard procedures, such as special frequencies, requests to use a specific approach procedure without communicating with the tower, or some such. These procedures are published in advance in the form of Notams and might, if devised early enough, also appear in the more popular aviation publications.

Although most of us, in the course of our normal flying activity, usually pay little attention to Notams, this is one instance when studying them in advance will pay divi-

Fig. 15-1. *Let's go to an air show!*

dends. Most FBOs are regular subscribers to Notams, and many will put the more important ones on their bulletin boards.

The following is a description of the procedure that was being used the last time I flew to the EAA Fly-In at Oshkosh—that particular time in a Cessna Turbo Centurion. Different procedures might be in effect during different years, but it illustrates why advance knowledge is of value.

When I was still some 50 miles out, too far to get any decent reception of the ATIS, I listened to Oshkosh Tower. There was relatively little chatter on that frequency, and every few minutes a voice came on, saying over and over:

> Aircraft arriving for the EAA Fly-In, do not contact the tower. Monitor 124.5 (it might have been another frequency, I don't remember) and follow instructions.

I turned to that setting when an apparently recorded voice gave these instructions:

> Aircraft arriving for the EAA Fly-In, do not contact the tower. Enter the downwind leg over the stone quarry northwest of the field and follow the aircraft in front of you. Monitor 118.7 (or whatever it was) for clearance to land. Do not transmit. You will be cleared to land when turning final.

This might not have been the exact wording, but basically it is what the instructions were.

Fig. 15-2. *The first problem would be to find that stone quarry.*

Because I was not familiar with the Oshkosh area, the first problem I had was to find the stone quarry (FIG. 15-2). I headed for some imaginary point northwest of the airport and, sure enough, I soon began to see airplanes of all types and sizes following one another downwind and, by searching the area from which they came, I eventually spotted my quarry. I headed for it and turned downwind behind a bright red experimental and ahead of an Aztec.

Once established in a situation like that, it is important to be proficient at slow flight because the airplane ahead might be doing just 60 or 70 knots, and overtaking him is strictly a no-no.

By now, listening to the other frequency that had been broadcast earlier, I could hear one aircraft after another being given landing clearance, usually not by number, but by type and color: "Green Cessna single turning final, cleared to land . . . Yellow Cherokee behind the green Cessna, continue approach . . . Red experimental, follow the yellow Cherokee . . ." and so on. It was a good system and worked just fine, the best part being that it eliminated the frustrating problem of getting a word in edgewise when the tower is excessively busy and you're inexorably coming closer and closer.

The last time I flew to the now-defunct Reading Air Show, the routine was different (FIG. 15-3). Listening to ATIS, we were told to contact Reading Tower on one of several different frequencies, depending on the direction from which we were com-

Fig. 15-3. *A by-gone era. Tie downs at the old Reading Air Show in Pennsylvania—still a good example of airplane parking at a major show.*

ing. The trouble was that there were scattered clouds with bases around 1,000 feet or so, and the visibility below the clouds, although said to be 3 miles, was, to put it charitably, lousy.

In addition to giving us the frequencies, the voice also stated that the airport would be closed to all arrivals and departures from such and such time to such and such time because of an air show. Looking at the clock on the panel of the Bellanca Super Viking I was flying, I saw that I had 30 minutes to get on the ground, or I'd be stuck with either hanging around in the air for several hours or going elsewhere to land and wait.

For some silly reason, every time I flew to Reading VFR I had difficulties finding that airport, and I understand from others that I wasn't alone. I tuned in the appropriate tower frequency and listened to the instructions being given other aircraft, which usually amounted to: ". . . downwind for Runway 36 (or whatever), report abeam the tower."

Somehow I didn't feel like calling them and announcing myself, not knowing how long it would take to find the airport. So I stayed above the scattered clouds where the visibility wasn't too bad and flew toward the airport, hoping that I'd see it once I got there.

Well, if I remember correctly, it was just about three minutes before the airport was supposed to be closed when I finally spotted the runway right beneath me between the clouds. "Reading Tower, Bellanca One Two Three Four Alpha, above the airport, with the numbers, landing."

"Bellanca Three Four Alpha, downwind for Runway three six, report abeam."

I pulled back the throttle, dropped gear and flaps, and banked sharply to see as much as possible beneath me, dropped down, managed to figure out which was the right runway, and somehow got myself established on downwind. I reported, was told to follow an Aerostar turning base, and finally got the clearance to land when I was about 100 feet from the threshold, maybe 10 or 15 feet above the ground.

Another example involves the time I flew to the air races at Cape May, New Jersey. I don't remember the exact routine being used at the time. What I do remember was being established on final when suddenly there appeared a twin below and overtaking me. Well, that's enough to give you momentary heart failure. Quite obviously, he never saw me at all, and I only saw him when he was far enough ahead of me to pose no further problem, assuming I could slow down my airplane, a Cherokee Six, to a speed that would permit me to land far enough behind him to not run into him before he had a chance to clear the runway. It all worked out fine, but in retrospect it is somewhat scary to think what would have happened if I had decided to steepen my descent while he was apparently directly below me.

In all of these situations, extreme vigilance is of major importance. There is no way for you to depend on tower controllers or whoever is handling the traffic on the ground to warn you of potential traffic conflicts. It's strictly a see-and-be-seen operation.

In addition, remember that such aviation events usually attract a great number of pilots who might only have a few hundred hours in their logbooks, and who might, therefore, be somewhat less efficient in heavy-traffic situations than the ones you usually encounter around busy hub airports. It turns out to be much like driving in traffic. You have to not only fly your own airplane, you have to be aware of everyone around you and be ready to take unexpected evasive action if someone suddenly makes an unexpected maneuver.

THE GET-AWAY

The other half of the coin involves getting away from those places. When the fly-in, air show, air race, or whatever is over, usually on the afternoon of the last scheduled day, everybody wants to get out of there in one great fat hurry. Thousands of pilots start their engines and everybody wants to be among the first to taxi out to takeoff.

Again, the routine used by the controllers varies among locations. Most of the time, the tower and ground control are entirely left out of this process. Instead, there are controllers on the ground waving flags, who first funnel the airplanes from the tiedown area to the taxiways and then to the takeoff end of the active runway. Here other controllers, also with flags, will wave one aircraft after the other off. In some places, such as Reading, where the runway is wide enough, two aircraft might be waved into position side by side and then be given takeoff clearance in quick succession, with the aircraft on the right expected to make a right turnout, and the one on the left expected to turn left.

Occasionally, especially at locations where only one aircraft can take off at a

Experimental Aircraft Association.

Fig. 15-4. *Today's big show, EAA's annual Oshkosh, Wisconsin, fly-in.*

time, the congestion is such that it might take as much as an hour or more to taxi out. In such instances, particularly on warm summer days, it is advisable to shut down the engine and to push the aircraft in order to avoid having the engines overheat, not to mention using considerable fuel.

Considering the huge amount of traffic being handled in an unconventional manner, it is surprising that mishaps are a rarity (FIG. 15-4). Most of the credit for this must necessarily go to the large numbers of pilots involved, who seem to behave consistently with all possible consideration for the other guy. That, then, is the secret word: if everyone is considerate of his fellow pilots and uses more than the usual amount of vigilance, flying to air shows can be a safe and enjoyable experience.

16
Tales of Five Rivers

THE EXPERIENCES RELATED IN THE NEXT FEW PAGES INVOLVE FIVE DIFFERENT parts of the country, five different rivers, five VFR pilots, and five single-engine aircraft. They are based on actual flights or attempted flights between Boise, Idaho, and Portland, Oregon; Seattle, Washington, and Portland, Oregon; Cincinnati, Ohio, and New York City; Cedar Rapids, Iowa, and Memphis, Tennessee; and Charlotte, North Carolina, and Washington, D.C. In all cases marginal weather and a river played an important part.

THE SNAKE RIVER

The first river in our anthology is the Snake River, the border between Idaho and Oregon, west and northwest of Boise. The pilot spent the night in Boise and planned to fly to Portland the next morning. His aircraft was a Cessna Skylane equipped with dual nav receivers, a transponder, and a simple Century I autopilot with VOR coupling capability.

When he got up in the morning, the weather in Boise was amply VFR despite a high broken overcast, occasional rain showers, and strong westerly winds, gusting occasionally to 30 knots. His route would take him from Boise along Victor 500 via Kimberly to south of Portland, where he would then turn north toward his destination (FIG. 16-1).

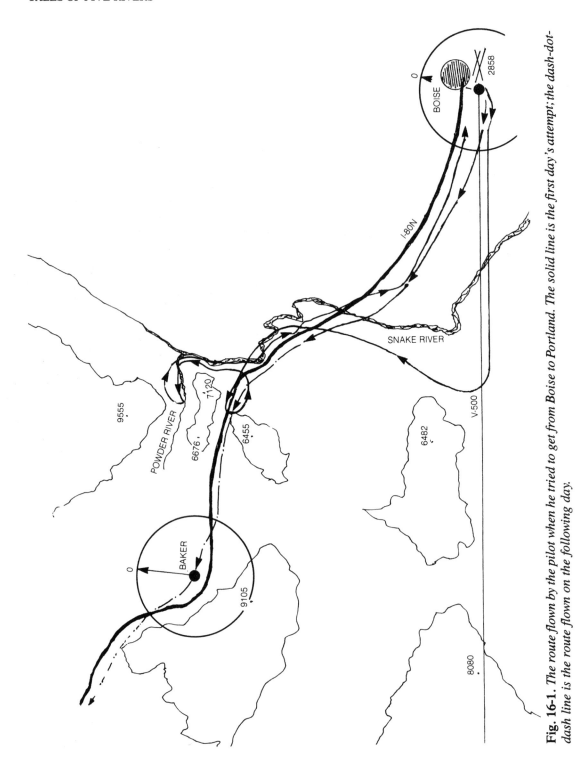

Fig. 16-1. *The route flown by the pilot when he tried to get from Boise to Portland. The solid line is the first day's attempt; the dash-dot-dash line is the route flown on the following day.*

Although this route looked rather simple on his Jepp chart, despite great distances between nav aids (Boise to Kimberly, 163 nm; Kimberly to Newberg, 145 nm), the MEAs are pretty high along that route: 11,000 for the first portion and 10,000 thereafter. A study of the Sectional charts shows the terrain along the way to be mountainous and devoid of populated areas or places to land in an emergency.

The reports and forecasts for the area involved talked of a frontal passage moving from the Pacific Northwest across the mountains southeasterly, with frequent low ceilings and mountaintops obscured. But the visibility figures weren't too bad.

Although he was aware that with the reported weather conditions he might not be able to make the flight as planned, he took off, figuring that there is always a 50−50 chance that the reports are worse than the actual conditions. The climbout from Boise, although bumpy, was uneventful. But even after he had leveled off at 6,500 feet, his ground speed was a depressing 95 knots based on the time it took to get to the point at which V-500 crosses the Snake River. Although the river itself and the terrain in the immediate vicinity is only about 2,500 feet or so, the mountains he would have to cross along his proposed route rise over 6,000 feet at first and eventually to over 9,000 feet.

By now he could clearly see that the weather straight ahead was hanging right down into the mountains, and there was no question that he would have to detour and try to find lower terrain if he were to make it without having to climb into IFR conditions (FIG. 16-2). The Jepp charts would be of no use in this attempt, so he spread the Sectionals on the seat to his right, annoyed by the fact that the only logical route avail-

Fig. 16-2. *The weather ahead was hanging right down into the mountains.*

able to him—following the Snake River as far as possible—lay on the edges and corners of three different charts, making chart reading in the bumpy airplane extremely difficult, even though the autopilot was, for the moment at least, doing the actual flying of the aircraft.

As best as he could figure out, he should be able to fly northward along the Snake to a point somewhere near a place called Huntington, where a major highway turned away from the river toward Baker. He should then be able to follow that highway to Baker and from there to Island City and Pendleton, where he'd intercept the Columbia River, which would take him straight into Portland. According to his chart, all of this should be possible at under 5,000 feet without hitting anything.

At first, everything went as planned. He flew north along the river, found the highway, and followed it for a few miles, only to find that the pass between 6,000 and

Fig. 16-3. *The pass ahead was obscured by low clouds and a horrendous rain shower.*

7,000-foot mountains, near a place called Durkee, was totally obscured by low clouds and a horrendous rain shower (FIG. 16-3). He contacted the Baker FSS, which reported a thunderstorm ahead with lightning in all quadrants. Obviously, this wasn't going to work.

He made a fast 180 and flew back along the highway until he got back to the Snake River. But he was still not ready to give up. According to the chart, some miles north of his position the Powder River runs into the Snake from the west, and he figured that there might just be a chance that by following first the Snake and then the Powder, he would be able to circumvent that pesky thunderstorm. So on he went, north along the Snake until he found the Powder where it turned left and followed it for a few miles in a westerly direction.

Throughout all of this time, the overcast above was intermittently broken, revealing towering buildups, which appeared to reach right up to jet altitudes, while the bases clung stubbornly to the tops of the higher mountains all around. It was kind of like flying in a tunnel—not a very comfortable experience—although the visibility itself remained ample below the clouds.

Well, the Powder River eventually fooled him, too. The same thunderstorm, or maybe a close relative, blocked the way in no uncertain terms, and there was just no alternative but to turn back. As much as he hated the idea of having wasted all that time, effort, and fuel, he decided that he would rather be around to fly again some other day, so he returned to Boise, checked back into the same Rodeway Inn, and relaxed for the rest of the day.

The front passed through Boise that night, drenching it with several inches of rain, but by morning the reports were considerably more encouraging, and he took off again. This time he made it, although the straight route along V-500 was still impossible VFR. But farther north, at Baker and beyond, the way he had attempted to go the day before, the clouds were scattered to occasionally broken, and he was able to climb in VFR conditions to an altitude above the clouds. To his left, along the more straight

Fig. 16-4. *Level at 1,000 feet over Puget Sound.*

line toward Portland, the tops still remained too high to be overflown without oxygen, but he eventually reached Pendleton, intercepted the Columbia River and followed it to Portland (FIG. 16-4).

THE NAMELESS CREEK

The second of our river adventures doesn't really involve a river at all, but rather an apparently nameless creek or rivulet, which has its origin somewhere to the north of Toledo, Washington, and runs southward into the Columbia River. The flight was to start at Boeing Field in Seattle and terminate at Troutdale Airport east of Portland, a total distance of only a little over 100 nm (FIG. 16-5). The aircraft was a Bellanca Super Viking equipped with dual navcoms, ADF, DME, transponder, and autopilot.

When it came time to leave Seattle, the weather was 1,500 feet overcast, visibility 5, with intermittent rain showers and occasionally lower ceilings reported for the route between Seattle and Portland. The pilot was an experienced VFR pilot with several thousand hours in his logbook and some instrument experience, but no instrument rating.

After he and a nonpilot passenger took off from Seattle, they leveled off at about 1,000 feet and flew across the southern portion of Puget Sound toward Olympia. So far, there was no serious problem, despite the low overcast. South of Olympia they followed the four-lane divided highway that runs more or less straight from there to Portland and remains at a fairly low elevation all the way, except in the vicinity of Toledo, where the terrain rises a few hundred feet. There seemed to be no good reason why they shouldn't be able to make Portland without difficulty.

It was after passing the Chehalis-Centralia Airport that things began to get a bit sticky. No matter how optimistic they would have liked to have been, there was no doubt that some miles ahead the highway and the base of the clouds were holding hands, a fact that was further emphasized by all those automobiles driving toward them with their headlights on.

Realizing that continuing on would be silly, they turned around and landed at Chehalis-Centralia to have a cup of coffee and figure out what to do next. While they were sitting at the counter in the coffee shop at the airport and discussing their predicament, a helpful local pilot told them about this little river, which more or less parallels the highway and which usually remains flyable when the highway itself is obscured.

They dragged out their charts and found that, true enough, if they followed the railroad tracks that ran right by the airport, they'd intercept something that looked on the chart like a tiny blue line, bordered on either side by a railroad and a road. Following it would take them eventually back to the major highway and to the bend in the Columbia River, which they could follow all the way to Portland.

They decided to try it, figuring that if it didn't work, they could always turn around again. They took off, picked up the railroad tracks and, after a while, found the little river. With the visibility below the clouds sufficient to permit them to be sure

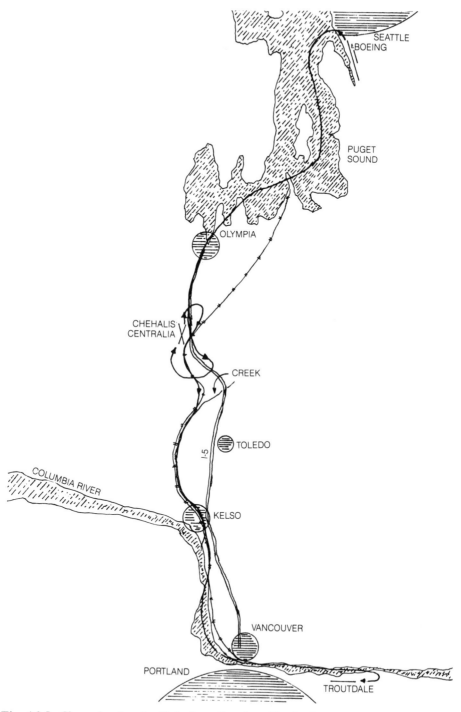

Fig. 16-5. *Chart showing the flight from Seattle to Portland.*

that there were no high-tension wires or other obstacles in the way, they stayed about 100 feet above the water, uncomfortably conscious that the terrain on both sides was obscured by clouds.

But it worked. They made it to the Columbia River and then followed it around that great bend that separates Portland, Oregon, from Vancouver, Washington, and all the way to the Troutdale Airport, where they had to request a special VFR clearance for landing because the ceiling was considerably less than 1,000 feet.

THE OHIO RIVER

The pilot had been at a business aircraft convention in Cincinnati. When it was over, he was asked by a friend if he was available to ferry a Cessna 172 to New York City, and the pilot agreed.

The distance from Cincinnati to New York is about 550 nm, which is well within the range of the Skyhawk, assuming flight at a reasonable altitude and with the mixture proportionately leaned. The original plan was to fly from Cincinnati via V-128 to Charleston, West Virginia, and from there via V-4 to Elkins and Kessel, then take V-166 to Martinsburg, Westminster, and New Castle, then V-157 and subsequently V-123 via Robbinsville to Teterboro Airport (FIG. 16-6)—all pretty cut and dried if the weather had been good or if the pilot had been instrument-rated. As it was, neither was the case.

The weather at Cincinnati on the day of departure was just barely VFR—a solid overcast around 3,000 feet and reported visibility of 3 miles, although it seemed considerably less. The pilot, with a student pilot passenger in the right seat, took off and headed south to pick up the 105-degree radial from the Cincinnati VOR (CVG), which coincides with V-128. Once on that radial he changed course and flew outbound on it, hoping to be able to continue receiving the VOR until he could pick up York (YRK), the next station along his route of flight, a distance of 84 nm. But it didn't work. The CDI needle began to shudder only too soon; the OFF flag popped up; and the needle went dead.

Now, except for the Ohio River, which runs somewhere south of the airway, the country looked rather featureless, with every mile looking like every other mile. He turned southward to pick up the river and use it as a guide, but by the time he got there, the ceiling appeared to have lowered considerably, and he decided that discretion would dictate landing at some airport to calmly figure out how to proceed. The airport he picked was Fleming-Mason, some short distance south of the river and, actually, only about 50 nm from where the trip had started.

Taking the appropriate charts with them, the pilot and his passenger settled down in the pilot lounge to assess the situation. When coming in for a landing at the airport, which is at a 915-foot elevation, the ceiling had been so low that it had actually been impossible to fly a regular pattern, and, as best as could be seen, to the east it looked just as bad, if not worse.

They spread out the charts on a big table and discussed the next move. According to the long-range forecasts, the weather would not improve to any meaningful degree

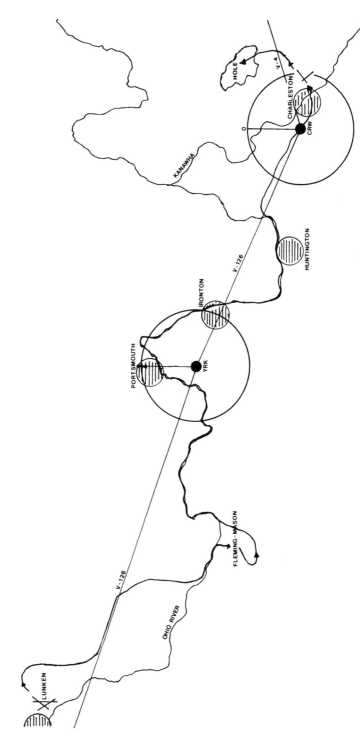

Fig. 16-6. *Chart showing the flight east from Cincinnati to Charleston and from there to VFR conditions on top.*

for at least a day, and neither man was particularly enamored of the idea of spending all that time in a motel, even if there had been one.

The alternative was to find the best way to continue eastward. The terrain to the east rises to around 1,500 feet, which, although certainly not high, was likely to be impossible considering the bases of the clouds in the area. But the Ohio River runs right through it at a much lower level, although its course is anything but straight. Still, they figured, they could take off, pick up the river, and follow it along its convoluted route via Portsmouth and Ironton to Huntington, West Virginia. There the river makes a sharp turn to the north, but with the terrain east of there at a somewhat lower elevation, they might just be able to pick up the four-lane highway and follow it eastward to Charleston.

From there, it was likely to get a little complicated. Another river, the Kanawha, comes to there from the southeast out of the Allegheny Mountains, which they knew they couldn't possibly expect to cross unless there was a break in the overcast somewhere, so they could climb out to VFR conditions on top. The alternative was a rather convoluted highway, which runs from Charleston along the western slopes of the Alleghenies through Clarksburg and on into Pennsylvania.

The longer they studied the charts, the more convinced they became that, although they could certainly make Charleston, there would be no alternative but to stay there and wait out the weather, unless they could obtain some information of improving conditions somewhere in the vicinity.

Looking at the charts didn't improve things, so they took off, picked up the river, and followed it religiously around its many bends and turns. It was strenuous flying, and even at their altitude—just a few hundred feet above the water—the visibility was barely sufficient to give them an idea of the next bend in the river before it was time to make the turn. But at least they weren't in the clouds, although whether these conditions could have been described as legally VFR is doubtful. Instinctively, both men kept leaning forward, as if that would improve their ability to detect power lines or any other obstructions that might have to be avoided.

After what seemed like an inordinate amount of time, they finally passed through Huntington. Seeing that the highway to their right appeared to be visible for at least a mile or so, they left the safety of the river and picked up the highway instead. By now, being within only about 35 nm of Charleston, the VOR (CRW) came in loud and clear, and they were overjoyed to hear of occasional breaks in the overcast. If that held up, maybe they could make it after all.

They landed at Charleston, refueled, and had a bite to eat. Then they visited the FSS and found that, true enough, there were breaks reported in the overcast not too far east, and pilot reports about cloud tops placed them at between 10,000 and 12,000 feet, while the New York area was forecasting scattered to broken conditions with adequate visibilities.

The rest of the flight, then, turned out just fine. Although those reported breaks were not exactly big, fat holes, but rather thin spots through which the sun and sky above were barely visible, they did manage to climb out without being illegal for more than a minute or so, and once on top they could finally pick up a straight route toward their destination.

THE MISSISSIPPI RIVER

The pilot who was sitting in Cedar Rapids, Iowa, and who finally ended up in Memphis, Tennessee, hadn't really wanted to go there at all. In fact, he was on his way home to southern California, but one of those immense summer warm fronts had settled and then stalled over the entire middle of the country—and no change was forecast for some time. Being a pilot and, therefore, impatient, he decided that hanging around and waiting didn't appeal to him. Instead, he would head south toward the Mississippi and follow it just as far as necessary to circumvent that warm front.

The Mississippi, of course, is a nice big river, which makes flying along it easy, even if the clouds hang relatively low all around (FIG. 16-7). And this is what he did. The aircraft was a Piper Comanche 250 with 90 gallons of fuel, which gave him ample range. So he just flew on and on, often less than 100 feet above the water, always keeping an eye out to the west in order not to miss any chance that might permit him to turn in that direction.

Fig. 16-7. *The Mississippi is a nice, big river, which makes flying along it easy.*

Fig. 16-8. *After that, it was down again, right onto the deck.*

But it never worked. Luckily, as he came close to the St. Louis metropolitan area, the ceiling did him a favor and lifted sufficiently to permit him to overfly all those bridges and the Gateway Arch, but then it lowered again, forcing him down to the deck until he arrived some 35 or 40 nm north of Memphis (FIG. 16-8). Suddenly, there was blue sky above and ahead, as if all that cloud deck had been cut with a knife.

He refueled in Memphis and got a bite to eat. Then he turned west toward Dallas and beyond, that awful warm front now lying to the north of his course.

THE JAMES RIVER

The pilot started off from Charlotte, North Carolina, with Washington, D.C., as his destination. He never got there on that flight, and if it hadn't been for a bit of dumb luck, he might never have gotten anywhere ever again.

The total distance is less than 300 nm, and although he was flying a Cessna 150, which isn't known for its great range, he should have been able to make that distance easily. Except, of course, nothing works that way.

The weather at Charlotte was amply VFR with a broken overcast at 5,000 feet and visibility better than 15 miles. He had been flying no more than 20 minutes when he decided that turbulence below the clouds didn't appeal to him and that he'd rather be up above, where it was bound to be smoother. So, picking a great, big blue spot between some of those broken clouds, he shoved the throttle all the way in and started up.

He was right. Once above the clouds and level at 9,500 feet, it was smooth and simply beautiful. The forecast weather for the Washington area was much like where he was—broken conditions with good visibilities—and he wasn't worried.

He had been flying like that for an hour when he realized that the undercast beneath him had become quite solid and that he hadn't had a glimpse of the ground for some time. He tuned his radio to Raleigh-Durham (RDU) and asked to be given the latest weather for Washington, expecting to be told that it was still as it had been advertised earlier.

"Washington, ceiling 2,000 overcast, visibility 3, light rain."

What had happened? Well, whatever had, if it continued, would mean he would never be able to get down safely from his current altitude. He asked if there was a chance for improvement during the next few hours and was told that, to the contrary, conditions were expected to deteriorate further. In that case, what was the nearest place with reports of broken conditions or better? He was asked to stand by, and after a pause, which seemed longer than it actually was, he was told that everything north of him was either IFR or at least covered by a solid overcast, with only Lynchburg, Virginia, reporting occasional breaks.

Lynchburg? Where is Lynchburg? He dug out his charts and eventually found it on his Cincinnati Sectional. So that was Lynchburg, right next to some 4,000-foot

Fig. 16-9. *He searched for the breaks in the clouds but couldn't find any.*

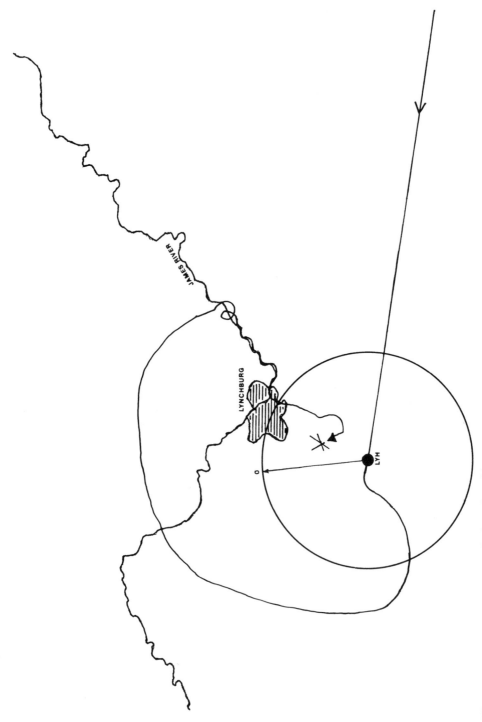

Fig. 16-10. *Chart showing the flight to Lynchburg.*

mountains and with the James River running right through it. Well, Lynchburg it was. He tuned his nav receiver to 109.2 and was gratified to have his OBI react immediately. After all, even though he still had about half his fuel, he didn't relish the idea of running low while looking for some of those occasional breaks, which, he hoped, would have the decency to stick around until he got there.

As he had many times before, he began wishing he was flying a faster airplane. Even though the distance from his present position to Lynchburg wasn't that great, it seemed to take forever. But finally, the CDI started to fluctuate and then the ambiguity meter changed from TO to FROM, meaning that he had just overflown the VOR.

But what about those breaks? He searched the undercast in all directions but could see nothing but solid clouds (FIG. 16-9). He called Flight Service while listening through the Lynchburg VOR and asked for the latest report, and he was told exactly what he'd heard earlier: 1,500 overcast, visibility 6, occasional breaks in the overcast.

Okay, so all he had to do was find those breaks. He decided to fly a wide circle around the VOR, turning first south, then west, then north, and so on, and, sure enough, there off to his right, was something that might just turn out to be what he had been looking for. He headed for it and when he got there what he saw was a tree-lined river below his wing. Without hesitation, he pulled back on the throttle and put the nose down toward that friendly piece of real estate. He had to do a bit of fancy twisting and turning to stay out of the clouds, but pretty soon he was over the river, with the bases of the clouds hanging low all around.

He knew, of course, that by following the river he would eventually get to Lynchburg, except he didn't know which way to follow the river. He could have kicked himself. Why hadn't he checked his VOR receiver before heading down so that he would know in which direction the station was from his current position? As it was, way down here in the riverbend between the hills, the VOR stubbornly refused to come in again. And, even though he was fairly certain that he was somewhere north of the city and the airport, that damned river was twisting and turning in all directions, and it did, in fact, turn north on both sides of town. Well, eenie, meenie, minee, moe . . . and he turned in the direction that seemed to him, for some reason, to be more logical than the other.

This is where dumb luck came in. As it turned out, he had picked the right direction. After about five or ten minutes of carefully following every turn in the river, there were some houses, and then some more, and even the OBI came back to life. After a bit of low-level searching he found the airport and was glad to finally be on the ground again, even though it wasn't where he had wanted to go (FIG. 16-10).

17
Tailwind I

IN LATER YEARS, THE FLIGHT WAS TO BE ONE TO TALK ABOUT TIME AND again in pilot lounges and drafty hangars. After all, how many pilots could claim to have covered 482 nm in 2 hours and 10 minutes in an airplane that had a normal cruise speed of 100 knots? It sounded more like a fairy tale, but it did, in fact happen.

It all started at El Paso on a windy spring day. The pilot, after preflighting his Cessna 175, removed the tiedown chains and started to taxi toward the active runway, firmly holding onto the yoke to prevent the rudder and ailerons from being buffeted by the strong, gusty wind.

Then came the first of several unexpected developments that day. At an intersection of several taxiways, he tried to make a 90-degree turn downwind, but the airplane simply wouldn't respond. No matter how hard he tried, it simply wouldn't turn the way he wanted. At first he couldn't figure out the reason, and then it occurred to him that the wind was pushing so hard against the vertical stabilizer that it made a turn in that direction impossible. Okay, if it wouldn't turn one way, maybe it would the other. So, instead of making a 90-degree turn to the right, he tried for a 270-degree to the left, and sure enough, the desired result was achieved.

At the takeoff end of the two-mile-long runway, he did his runup, checked the controls, and called the tower, which cleared him for takeoff. With the wind right on his nose, he seemed to be lifting off before he really had a chance to get moving, but the airplane was safely airborne and climbing the way it should.

His takeoff had been on Runway 26, so now, with his destination Waco, Texas, with a planned fuel stop in Midland, he started his turn toward the east, at the same time calling FSS to ask them to activate his VFR flight plan. Halfway through the turn he looked at the ground and was aware of being blown sideways across the ground, but eventually he was lined up and on course toward the east, cursing under his breath because he was getting bounced around something fierce.

GETTING ABOVE THE TURBULENCE

Although he had accumulated several hundred hours in the airplane, he had not yet reached the stage where he would accept uncomfortable turbulence with equanimity. Instead, whenever things got rough, he would climb to higher and higher altitudes under the assumption that things might get smoother up there. Most of the time this does prove to be the case, but on this day it didn't seem to work.

He was already climbing through 10,000 feet and still the turbulence refused to abate. There were some scattered to occasionally broken clouds just above him, and he decided to try to get on top of them, hoping that might do the trick. Although he had no oxygen on board, he had often spent considerable time at 14,000 or 15,000 feet without any more ill effects than a slight headache.

At 13,500 feet he was finally on top of the clouds, for all the good that climbing had done him. It was still rough, so he knew he'd just have to try to relax and enjoy it. Obviously, this was going to be just one of those days.

He had opened his flight plan at 10:30 A.M. Mountain Standard Time, or to be more professional, at 1730 Zulu, and had figured his time en route to Midland as 2 hours and 10 minutes. The climb to his present altitude had taken 33 minutes at an airspeed considerably below his normal cruise, so he would probably be late. As soon as he could reach Midland VOR he would call and tell them to extend his flight plan by some 15 or 20 minutes. There was plenty of time; he was certainly still well beyond reception distance.

He was still receiving the El Paso VOR and was navigating outbound on the appropriate radial, which he knew would take him via Salt Flat and Wink to Midland. Looking down at the West Texas landscape, which offers few landmarks other than the Guadalupe Mountains just east of Salt Flat, he was surprised to notice that the mountains were not where he had expected them to be. But then, after all, he could only see portions of the ground through the spaces between the clouds, so he was most probably mistaken. Still, just to make sure, he tuned in the Salt Flat VOR.

When the ambiguity meter in the OBI produced a FROM rather than TO reading, he briefly thought that maybe there was something wrong with the nav receiver. He played around with it for a while, tuning in other VORs in the area, Hudspeth and Carlsbad, only to find that either something was completely crazy, or that he was much farther along than could reasonably have been expected. Well, he might as well try Midland and see if he could receive them. Sure enough, not only did Midland come in loud and clear, but if his OBI wasn't lying to him, he was practically there already.

AMAZING JOURNEY

How could that be? By now he'd been airborne for just over an hour, and the distance from El Paso to Midland was, after all, over 200 nm. How could he have covered that much ground in so short a time in an airplane that had never before managed to cruise at better than 100 knots? Maybe it wasn't possible, but there was a big opening between the clouds, and just below him and to the left he couldn't fail to recognize the Midland Regional Airport. He'd been there often enough before to know exactly what it looked like. Okay, so maybe he was flying a jet and didn't know it. Anyway, he called Midland and told them to cancel his VFR flight plan, saying that at his apparent current ground speed he had ample fuel on board to continue on nonstop to Waco.

Throughout the rest of the flight, he was so busy marveling at the unbelievable story that his nav receiver insisted on telling him, as he tuned from one VOR to the next, that he practically forgot to be annoyed at the ride, which never had abated. Exactly 2 hours and 10 minutes after liftoff, his wheels touched down on Runway 23 at Waco.

Still somewhat disbelieving about what had happened during the past two hours, he went up to the tower to see if those guys might have a solution to the puzzle.

"Hi."

"Hi. Listen, did you guys move Waco from where it used to be?" he asked.

"Not that I know of. Why?"

"I just came from El Paso in a Cessna 175, which cruises at 100 knots and it took me 2 hours and 10 minutes. It just doesn't make sense."

"How high did you fly?"

"Pretty high. It was bumpy, so I climbed up to 13,500 and stayed up there all the way."

"That explains it."

"How come?"

"We've got a freak jetstream situation today. It's way down low."

"You mean, I've been flying in the jetstream?"

"Seems that way. We've had reports of winds up to 150 knots as low as 15,000 feet."

"Heavens! It's darn lucky I wasn't going the other way. I'd have been flying backwards."

This then was the tailwind, which for years to come would make up for hours and hours of headwinds, and which was to become the subject of much hangar talk.

18
Tailwind II

WHEN THE PILOT AWOKE THAT MORNING, HE WAS DISCOURAGED BY THE lack of sunlight coming through the window because that probably meant there was a heavy overcast outside. Sure enough, clouds hung overhead with a stiff north wind blowing, but thankfully, there was neither rain nor other precipitation that could hinder visibility.

Naturally, he had to be back in the office the next day for some important work, and he wondered if he should return that day or wait one day. He called Flight Service to see if the clouds were local, hoping they would dissipate by the estimated time of departure that afternoon.

The forecast wasn't good, but it wasn't bleak, either. Clouds covered the area for several hundred miles around, including his direction of flight, and they were not expected to break up for at least 24 hours. However, it was only an overcast with no rain, fog, or other hindrance to visibility, which, in fact, ranged from 10 to 20 miles along the route. The wind was 20 to 30 knots from the north and he was flying south, so there would at least be a tailwind.

If the forecast held, it would be a legal VFR flight, but it would be at a very low altitude. Fortunately, it was a very familiar route for the pilot, who had learned to fly over the first half of the route and covered the second half twice a month on business. He had memorized highways, cities, lakes, power lines, and other landmarks, along with the most important element: airport locations.

But it was a familiar route from several thousand feet at cruise altitudes. How would it be at traffic pattern altitudes? Go/no-go? Probably go, but wait until early afternoon and check the weather again.

GETTING APPREHENSIVE

By lunch time, the local weather had not changed, and the pilot was getting slightly apprehensive. Flight Service reported some breaks in the clouds to the north, but along his route of flight conditions were unchanged—good visibility with a tailwind. Based on that information, the pilot filed a VFR flight plan and prepared to leave.

To complement his knowledge of the route, he took time to closely examine the Sectional chart, targeting airports that could become safe refuges if conditions worsened. Fuel would be no problem, so if the weather held it would be a nonstop flight. Go/no-go? By now it was "go"—to the airport—and he was on the way.

His apprehension was allayed en route to the airport when sunlight punched through the overcast here and there. Airspace illuminated by the sun below the clouds was crystal clear—no moisture to hinder visibility. Buffeted by the north wind, he loaded the airplane, preflighted, and went inside to check the weather one last time before taking off. Flight Service reported no change for better or worse—"go."

Once airborne, he took up a heading that would lead him to the route's major dogleg, and he climbed to find the ceiling high enough to cruise nearly 1,000 feet above the ground. Leveled out, he took stock of the situation—aircraft performing well, good visibility, some minor bumps, and what appeared to be a great ground speed—and relaxed. For the moment, everything was okay, and if it deteriorated rapidly, he could simply turn back and try again the next day.

Primary checkpoints came up quickly and were right on target with little course correction, so he was riding a direct tailwind. His "lifeline" for the first leg of the flight appeared quickly, and he relaxed some more. The major four-lane highway would take him directly to the dogleg turn, and he was right on top of it. His earlier apprehension gave way to enjoyment of some unseen sights when flying the route at higher altitudes. Then the navigation system came to life, receiving the VOR representing the dogleg's joint.

RAPID CHANGES

The pilot was again taking stock of the situation when he realized that it was getting darker. Obviously the overcast was getting thicker, but he could still see more than 10 miles underneath, so he wasn't worried. Then he realized how the clouds were getting thicker: they were getting lower. He had to drop down several hundred feet to avoid them. Thankfully, the ceiling leveled out and forward visibility was holding, so the clouds did not drop to the surface.

Approaching the VOR, it was time for an en route go/no-go decision. The flight was progressing better than expected; thanks to the tailwind, he was at least 15 minutes ahead of schedule, compared to other trips. The aircraft was performing flawlessly. Visibility was still excellent. Fuel was fine. The only worry was the cloud cover—and the question of whether or not it would hold or drop lower.

A quick visit with Flight Service revealed good visibility at the destination, with no rain or fog reported along the remainder of the route, and it appeared the ceiling did not change much. The pilot's first en route decision was to keep going.

Negotiating the dogleg would be tricky. He wanted to approach the VOR and establish his heading FROM the station before arriving at the station. But a busy airport near the VOR would prevent that. He flew TO the station at his current heading and made the right-hand dogleg turn just prior to arriving over the VOR site that he could see. All of a sudden, he realized it had gotten darker again, and he was gradually descending to avoid the cloud deck, but he got on his radial and verified it with references to his compass and directional gyro. He waited for a new road to appear.

He knew that at such a low altitude VOR reception would be lost soon, and he had to be over the road that would keep him on course. Here came a road, and comparing it to the Sectional, it appeared to be the one he needed, so he made the course correction and started following it.

He was beginning to get apprehensive again. He had driven on the road he wanted to follow, but this road had no familiar landmarks, like houses or gas stations.

He decided to hold his heading and see where the road went, hoping it would soon become familiar. Turning back never crossed his mind at this point. He was ahead of schedule and wanted to be home, not halfway. However, it would get worse before it got better.

He was over the wrong road, and by now it had twisted and curved until he was heading north, 90 degrees perpendicular to his intended route. He quickly decided to make a 180-degree turn to intersect the road he wanted to follow. For a moment, he was "disoriented," but he could always take up a heading that would go back to the VOR's reception area and start from there again, so the pilot continued searching for his east-west highway.

LOOKING FOR A LAKE

Flying due south, now he was over a north-south road that hopefully would intersect his highway. According to the Sectional, a lake would be visible south of the roadway's intersection, so that made for a bona fide checkpoint. He continued looking, but there was no lake or any major intersections. Then his north-south road stopped.

Apprehension finally gave way to real fear—he was lost. He flew a crude figure eight, hoping to spot a water tower, town, or, best of all, an airport, but there was nothing, just pasture land. Attempts to raise any VOR were futile; he was too low.

His first decision was the smartest he could make: *Think*; take up a straight and level course that will at least head in the correct direction toward home; settle down and think some more. He needed someplace to fly to, a specific place that would ideally get him back on course, or at least have an airport where he could land and take stock of the situation. The worst-case scenario would be to climb and hope the overcast was thin enough to break out on top and take it from there.

He scanned the horizon, but it remained barren. He took a deep breath and decided to examine the Sectional. Considering the major course corrections he had made earlier—wrong course corrections—he mentally drew a box where he was probably located. Scanning the chart, he looked for "help" in the area around the box. He spotted something . . . maybe it would work.

A small airport he had flown over many times before had a nondirectional beacon (NDB) that just might be strong enough to receive, wherever he was. Quickly tuning the automatic direction finder (ADF), the audible Morse Code identifier filled the cockpit and the needle swung hard, locking on the signal. Relief—someplace to fly to, and it would get the trip right back on course!

Established on course to the NDB, the pilot did a fast analysis, and found he was far south of the intended track that would have been to the west. After the VOR dogleg, he apparently followed a highway that turned north, instead of running west. Then his road that ran south was not the road near the lake—he had flown past the intended east-west highway while looking for the lake.

BACK ON COURSE

Approaching the NDB and spotting the airport, he wanted to land and take a breather, but the weather was holding, fuel and aircraft were fine, and he was starting to settle down—he knew exactly where he was and exactly how to get home. Also, three airports would be right on course and a fourth off-course airport would be visible if needed. Still "go."

Like clockwork, the flight continued. The ceiling even seemed to lift some, and the pilot tuned the ADF to receive the AM broadcast station at home. It came in loud and clear.

He would remain over major highways until about 30 miles away from the destination airport, then it would be up to the airplane's ADF to point the way home. He passed two of the three airports and he approached the third. Time for another tough decision: land at the third airport and call for a ride home, or continue? He considered critical aspects of the flight: visibility was excellent, the plane had plenty of fuel, the ceiling had not dropped any lower, there was no turbulence, the ADF was working flawlessly. Directly over the last airport he made the decision: continue. He had no suspicion of what was about to sneak up on him.

THE MICROWAVE TOWER

Relying solely on the ADF and the broadcast station, he was right on course for home. The pilot glanced over his shoulder and looked at the last airport as it disappeared. When he turned around, the cloud deck seemed to drop all of a sudden. He descended slightly and looked forward to be sure the good visibility was holding. It was fine, but the cloud-to-ground distance seemed to be deteriorating. Were the clouds lowering, or was the terrain rising?

The aircraft was too low for a quick turn back to the last airport, and by now the ADF was receiving the home airport's NDB, so he continued the flight. The terrain had risen, but it leveled out and familiar roads fell into place under the aircraft. The pilot knew he was extremely low. He rarely glanced at the altimeter, more concerned with staying away from the ground—and a microwave tower in the area.

He knew the tower was on the left side of the road he was flying over. And the ADF was pointing left of course to the airport, so he made a 45-degree right turn, heading for the airport and watching for the tower. Thankfully, it appeared on the right side, and the plane passed by at least a mile away.

Now the only thing lying between the aircraft and the airport was his hometown. Ideally, the pilot would skirt the city, approaching the airport from the southeast or northeast, but there were power transmission lines south of the airport and radio towers on the north. He would have to fly very low over the southern part of the city. There were no major obstacles, but he was sensitive to noise created by the airplane, so he reduced power for a quiet overflight. And by flying over that section of town, he could safely glide to one of several pastures in an emergency, away from homes and businesses.

Finally, the uncontrolled airport appeared with the windsock indicating the same stiff north wind that had been present at departure. The pilot crossed over the airport at midfield and entered the prescribed right downwind that kept traffic away from the city. Abeam the touchdown zone he reduced power, kept his landing pattern close, since he was already so low, crossed the numbers and touched down—safely home.

REVELATIONS

He taxied up to the fuel pump, pulled the mixture back, and breathed a tremendous sigh of relief as the prop jerked to a stop. A quick call to Flight Service canceled his flight plan.

Only then did the pilot realize what time it was. Usually, the trip averaged $2^1/2$ hours. This trip, from wheels off to wheels down, had taken just 2 hours. A remarkable trip, but imagine how fast it would have been without the deviations. Closing the hangar doors, the pilot completely relaxed as he latched the padlock.

He looked up at the clouds for the first time since landing. He paused to think: if he were opening the doors instead of closing them, would he fly in the prevailing weather conditions? Probably not.

19
Panic!

IT WAS LATE AFTERNOON. DARK CLOUDS RIMMED BY THE GOLDEN LIGHT OF the lowering sun were gathering overhead. A storm, which had been building for days over the Pacific south of Alaska, was creeping inland across the Siskyou Mountains and Trinity Alps of northern California, spilling its clouds between tall peaks toward Red Bluff and into the valley that lies protected between the Sierra Nevada and the coastal mountain range.

The forecast for the area called for ceilings of less than 1,000 feet and visibilities of less than 3 miles, with light to moderate rain showers. Conditions were expected to continue throughout the evening and into the night.

There were still specks of blue sky above, fringed with the orange of sunset between the billowing cumulus (FIG. 19-1). For a brief moment, the golden shape of a sunlit Mooney moved across, disappearing again behind the fast-moving clouds. From its vantage point, the sky was a fairyland of deceiving beauty (FIG. 19-2). Colors ranged from aquamarine to deep purple. In the west, where mountains topping the clouds tried to reach for the heavens, the golden sun played hide and seek.

However, the pilot of the Mooney was not in the mood to contemplate beauty. Caught on top, he found himself pulling his airplane somewhat erratically around the towering buildups, his eyes desperately searching for a glimpse of the ground, a hole in the undercast large enough to permit him to get down (FIG. 19-3). Racing with what

Fig. 19-1. *Looking up, he could still see specks of blue sky.*

Fig. 19-2. *The sky above glowed with the evening light.*

Fig. 19-3. *With no horizon to guide him, he instinctively increased back pressure.*

seemed to him to be incredible speed between gold-white-purple-black ever-moving shapes that threatened to swallow him and his airplane, he began to realize that he no longer had any clear idea of his present position.

"I wonder how high the mountains are around here?" Like so many pilots who often fly alone, he tended to do his thinking out loud.

"How high am I? Over 12,000 feet. That's good. There couldn't be anything that high." He looked at the gauges. "At least there's still enough fuel. Maybe not an awful lot, but enough to get me down."

His radio, tuned to the Red Bluff VOR, suddenly came to life. "Roger, seven three Tango, canceling your VFR flight plan. Latest Red Bluff weather 1,800 broken, 2,500 overcast, visibility 3, light rain, wind light and variable, altimeter 28.83. Do you have the airport in sight?" Pause. "There is no reported traffic."

The pilot breathed a sigh of relief. "That's the place to go. They're VFR and it has to be down there someplace." He centered the CDI needle, obtaining a 243-degree reading and a TO indication.

Suddenly it was dark in the cockpit. He looked up. "Shucks." He was in the clouds. His hands automatically tightened on the yoke as turbulence bounced him first up, then down. "I wish I had an autopilot. What's that everybody keeps saying? Never mind the seat of the pants, just watch the instruments—airspeed, artificial horizon! How come it's slowing down? Ninety-five, ninety. . . . Push that nose down! Ahhh . . ."

Suddenly there was light again in the cockpit. He was once more in the clear. The sky above still glowed with the evening light, a star appearing here and there. But all around, right, left, in front, and behind, as far as he could see, immense buildups were reaching toward the heavens.

I'VE GOT TO GET DOWN

He banked, circling to try and stay in the clear, and with no horizon to guide him he instinctively increased back pressure, as if by climbing steeper and steeper, he could outmaneuver the clouds. A stall warning beeped briefly and erratically, and he pushed the yoke forward. "I've got to get down through this stuff." He tried to remember what had been said about the ceiling at Red Bluff, but he couldn't. He picked up the mike.

"Red Bluff Radio, Mooney three four two Whiskey Alpha."

"Two Whiskey Alpha, Red Bluff."

"What's your weather down there?"

"Stand by."

Why don't these people simply look out the window? Stand by! I can't stand by!

"Two Whiskey Alpha, Red Bluff reporting 1,200 scattered, 1,800 broken, 2,400 overcast, light rain. Visibility 3."

"Roger."

"Two Whiskey Alpha, what is your present position?"

To heck with my present position. None of your business! He tried to hang the mike back on its hook, but failed as turbulence bounced him around and he simply hung it over the right yoke.

"Two Whiskey Alpha, do you read Red Bluff?"

Forget it! I'm not going to have the FAA jump all over me for coming down through this stuff without an instrument ticket!

Right then, he was moving toward an immense cloud straight ahead of him, which, like some undulating prehistoric monster, blocked his way. With all the self-control he could muster, he concentrated on the airspeed indicator and artificial horizon, trying to ignore his increasing inner tension as all visual contact with the outside world disappeared.

He quickly glanced at the OBI. "What happened?" The needle had pegged. Hesitantly, he took one hand off the yoke and turned the OBS knob. The needle flipped to the other side, then slowly centered. The OBI indicated 183 degrees, but his directional gyro said 275 degrees. He would have to turn if he wanted to locate himself over the station. "Shallow, shallow turns!"

And then he saw the flag. It read FROM. "Oh, no!" Again he twisted the OBS knob until he got a TO indication and the needle returned to center with a 361-degree reading. "Think, man, think. That means that I'm south of Red Bluff and I'm going to have to turn again, north! What happened to that airspeed? It's down again."

He tried to relax the back pressure on the yoke, tried hard to think which way to turn in order to head north. "And why is that magnetic compass flipping around? Why doesn't it show the same thing as the DG? I've got to make sure the DG is right, but how? Straight and level, that's it. Come on now, straight and level!"

And then turbulence hit full force.

I DON'T KNOW WHERE I AM

In the muted calm of the Red Bluff Flight Service Station, the two men were relaxed.

"Whatever happened to Two Whiskey Alpha?"

"Beats me. I called a couple of times, but he didn't answer."

"Think he's in trouble?

"Maybe yes, maybe no. Didn't sound too relaxed, but then in this kind of weather, a lot of 'em get a bit nervous."

"Why don't you call him again?"

"Sure, why not?" His foot pressed on the contact bar, activating the mike. "Mooney two Whiskey Alpha, this is Red Bluff, do you read Red Bluff?"

Nothing.

"Or maybe he's simply turned his radio off or switched frequencies. Mooney two Whiskey Alpha, do you read Red Bluff? Over."

They waited.

"Forget it."

"I guess so." He unwrapped a somewhat soggy ham on rye and bit into it. "Sometimes I think I'll get married again, just so she can make decent sandwiches."

"You don't know when you're well off."

"Red Bluff! Red Bluff!" The voice that suddenly shouted through the speaker was slurred, trembling.

"Aircraft calling Red Bluff, go ahead." He shoved the sandwich aside. "I'll bet that's the Mooney."

"This is Mooney two Whiskey Alpha. I don't know where I am. Can you get me out of here?"

Six miles above the terrain a United Airlines DC-8 was passing over Oakland, flying from Los Angeles to Seattle.

"You take it," the captain told the copilot while turning up the sound on the number three com radio until the voice came in loud and clear.

"Mooney two Whiskey Alpha, this is Red Bluff. Are you on an IFR flight plan?"

"No, I'm on no flight plan at all. I need . . . ah . . . help."

"Right. Are you VFR now?"

"I haven't got any idea where I am. I've got to get out of this fog. I can't see a thing."

"Are you transponder equipped?"

"Am I what?"

"A transponder—do you have a transponder in the airplane?"

"Oh, transponder. No, I don't have a transponder."

By now, others were gradually becoming involved in the drama-in-the-making. Not only was the United captain listening in his perch way above all the weather, but Red Bluff also had contacted Oakland Center, asking them to try to establish radar contact. Oakland, in turn, informed the pilot of an Aztec at 4,000 feet on an IFR flight plan from Sacramento to Red Bluff to be prepared to hold because of an aircraft in trouble.

"What kind of trouble?"

"We don't know exactly. Red Bluff says it's a VFR pilot somewhere in the clouds. He doesn't know where he is."

"Oh, lovely! That's all I need. Anybody know his altitude?"

"We're trying to find out. Stand by."

In the cockpit of the Mooney, the pilot had opened all the vents, but perspiration was still pouring down his face. He kept hearing voices coming at him through the speaker, but he couldn't really comprehend what they wanted from him. "If they'd only stop talking and do something!"

"Mooney two Whiskey Alpha, Oakland Center wants you to call them on 120.4. They have radar there and they'll be able to help you."

"What was that? I don't understand."

"Oakland Center, they want you to switch your radio to 120.4 and give them a call. One-two-zero-point four!"

"Oh, right. 120.4. I'll try."

It seemed incredibly difficult to operate the knobs on the radio, and he had to keep wiping the perspiration from his eyes to be able to see, but eventually he did manage to switch to the new frequency.

"Oakland . . . ah . . . Center, this is Mooney . . . ah . . . two . . . ah . . . Whiskey Alpha."

"Two Whiskey Alpha, this is Oakland. What is your present position and altitude?"

"I couldn't hear . . . ah . . . what's that you want me to do?"

"What is your present position and altitude?"

"I don't know. I don't know where I am." He tried to read the altimeter through the perspiration. "I think it's like three thousand feet . . . no, more like thirty-five hundred."

"Roger. Climb to and maintain 6,000. I repeat, climb to and maintain 6,000. There are mountains all around you and you're below terrain-clearance altitude. Climb to six thousand."

"Six thousand. Okay, I'll try." He advanced the throttle as far as it would go and tried not to pull too hard on the yoke.

"What's your present heading?"

"I'm flying . . . I can't . . . just a minute. . . ." Again he wiped his eyes, trying to clear the blurred image of the DG. "I'm flying thirty degrees . . . yes . . . ah . . . thirty . . . west, that is, west."

"Roger. Remain on this frequency."

The United captain had switched to the Oakland frequency and followed the conversation, wishing that whoever was doing the talking at Oakland would be a bit more patient. His thoughts went back some 20 years and to how scared he had been the first few times he flew in real weather.

The Oakland voice came back on. "How much fuel do you have left?"

"Ah, what?"

"Fuel. Look at your fuel gauges. How much fuel have you got left?"

"Ah . . . about a third, it looks like."

"How much is that in hours?"

"Oh, I don't know. An hour maybe, Forty-five minutes."

"Roger."

During the ensuing pause, the United captain was tempted to pick up the mike and tell that poor soul that with 45 minutes of fuel in his tanks there was plenty of time and just to relax. But he didn't. Another voice might only add to the fellow's confusion.

"I still don't know where I'm at. I just don't know." The voice sounded high-pitched, desperate, as if choked with tears.

FLYING INTO THE MOUNTAINS

At Oakland Center, the usually relaxed atmosphere had changed. They had a problem and they all knew it.

"If he's actually flying thirty degrees like he says, he's flying right into the mountains."

"I know. And three hundred is not much better, and neither, for that matter, is west. We've got to get him turned south, away from the high terrain."

"Try again. At least he seems to have the airplane more or less under control. Maybe, if we can get him to make a turn, we can pick him up on radar."

"Mooney two Whiskey Alpha, Oakland Center."

"Ah . . . I'm here."

"What is your present heading?"

"My present . . . ah, I'm going on a heading of . . . ah . . . twenty degrees."

"Roger. Is that zero two zero?"

"What heading do you want me to go on?"

"Two Whiskey Alpha, are you on a heading of zero two zero?"

"I'm heading at the present time . . . ah . . . zero. . . ." There was a burst of static, then nothing.

For some time, the Aztec had been patiently flying a holding pattern, glad that the assigned altitude had turned out to be between layers, where he would at least have a chance to see the Mooney if it should, by any chance, come his way. He, too, had been listening to the Oakland Center frequency, and when there was no further word from the Mooney, he couldn't help wondering if "zero" would prove to have been the pilot's last word.

"This is . . . ah . . . Whiskey Alpha. I still don't know where I am."

The Aztec pilot breathed a sigh of relief.

"Two Whiskey Alpha, Oakland Center. What is your present heading and altitude?"

Again the Mooney failed to answer.

"Two Whiskey Alpha, request your present heading and altitude."

"I'm . . . ah . . . flying at . . . twenty-nine degrees."

"Roger."

By now the United captain felt certain that he could do better. He picked up the microphone, switching it to the No. 3 transmitter. Carefully keeping his voice calm and his speech slow and distinct, he depressed the button. "Mooney two Whiskey Alpha, this is a United Airlines jet high above you. Could you try to tell me where your think you are?"

"I . . . I have no idea."

"Where did you take off from and how long ago was that?"

"I took off from Seattle. That was about three and a half hours ago, I think." And then, after a pause, "I was going to San Francisco."

The captain, who had flown Mooneys himself, looked at his chart to try and figure out how far the Mooney might have flown at what he estimated its cruising speed to be. As best as he could guess, he should be over the valley in the Red Bluff area, all right, and there were high mountains in all directions except to the south. "If that's so, that puts you somewhere right in the vicinity of Red Bluff. In what direction are you flying right now? Can you tell me that?"

"I'm still climbing. I'm over 5,000 feet and I'm still climbing."

At this point the Oakland controller came back on the line. "Roger two Whiskey Alpha."

"What do you want me to do? How high do you want me to go here?"

The captain had to assume that Oakland preferred to handle things themselves, so he kept quiet.

"Mooney two Whiskey Alpha, Oakland Center. The MEA at your approximate position is . . . stand by." There was what seemed to all those listening a long pause. "Mooney two Whiskey Alpha, Oakland Center. Climb to and maintain 8,000."

"This is two Whiskey Alpha. I think I'm . . . ah . . . above the fog."

"You're above the clouds. Do you have visual contact at all?"

"No, I have no contact. . . ."

TELL ME WHAT TO DO

For a moment the Mooney pilot saw things. A patch of what seemed like sky, dimly lit outlines of clouds, but it didn't last. "If they'd only tell me what to do!"

He pressed the mike button. "I'm at 5,000 and I'm heading south about . . . ah . . ." He leaned forward to better see the DG. "About . . . ah . . . five degrees."

"Mooney two Whiskey Alpha, say again your present heading. This is Oakland. Say again your present heading."

"I'm . . . I'm heading south, I tell you . . . south, three degrees."

He pressed his fist against his eyes, then tried to wipe a nonexistent film from the face of the compass. "If only those people down there would stop asking questions! Why don't they just tell me what to do?" Suddenly he glanced at the artificial horizon and reacted with shock, seeing it steeply angled. He tried to level the wings, but it seemed to take much more effort than it should have.

"Two Whiskey Alpha, Oakland. I understand you're turning southbound from thirty degrees. Is that correct?"

The figure 3 seemed to eerily be swinging back and forth in front of him. "Three . . . three degrees."

"Roger. What is your present, I repeat, your present heading?"

He looked out of the window as if that solid wall of nothing could somehow miraculously provide the answer. "My present heading?" He tried to make sense out of the DG, then the magnetic compass, but the meaning of all those figures suddenly seemed to have escaped him. "I'm . . . I'm going pretty near due east . . . due west . . . three degrees." Totally exhausted, he dropped the mike into his lap. "I don't know where I'm going," he muttered, but no one heard him.

"We're trying to get a fix on you now, over."

Without bothering to pick up the microphone, he pleaded into nothingness, "Just tell me what to do. Please, just tell me what to do."

At the Oakland Center, the group around the controller working the wayward Mooney had grown.

"Do you have any idea where that Mooney is or where he's headed?"

"He says he's headed east."

"I thought he said west."

"Yeah, last he said west. I don't think he knows which way he's headed." Exasperated, he picked up the mike once more. "Mooney two Whiskey Alpha, can you give me your present heading?"

"North, I'm headed north."

One of the men watching the radar screen pointed and spoke up. "What about that one, 20 miles south of Red Bluff?"

"Could be. Could be anyone VFR on top or even below. How do we know?"

"How about making him fly some turns?"

"I'll try anything, but the way he sounds, I doubt he knows whether he's turning or not."

From one of the others standing by, "I don't know about turns. If he's hand-flying on instruments, we could make him lose control altogether."

The United captain, hearing the knock, released the lock on the cockpit door to admit one of the stewardesses who was bringing coffee.

"Here you are." She handed cups to each of the crew.

"I still have no idea where I'm at." Even the stewardess recognized the desperation in that voice coming over the speaker. "Trouble?"

"Some poor slob down there in the clouds. Oakland's been trying to find him."

Shaking her head, she turned to leave just as the Oakland voice came on again. "Two Whiskey Alpha, your compass heading. Can you give me your compass heading? You're flying by a compass, you have a compass in front of you. Now if you'll just take a good look at that and tell me what it says."

There was a very long pause and the captain was about to pick up the mike again when he finally answered.

"I'm flying due west."

"Roger. That's two seven zero compass heading, is that right?"

"I believe that's what it is. It's fog. I'm still in the fog. I'm at seven thousand feet and I'm still in the fog."

"Roger. Can you climb some more? You should break out on top at approximately nine thousand feet."

"Got you. I'm climbing out."

The captain still felt there might be some help he could give. He pressed the mike button. "Mooney two Whiskey Alpha, do you read United?"

"I read you . . . but I've no idea what I'm doing."

"Two Whiskey Alpha, Oakland. We believe we now have you in radar contact, approximately 45 miles south-southwest of Red Bluff. Can you take a heading of zero eight five for about two minutes? Over."

The captain now switched the mike to the radio, which was tuned to one of the other center frequencies. "Center, United three eight eight."

"Go ahead, United."

"I believe if you ask him to just take cardinal headings like, uh, east, it'll probably be a little easier for him to understand at this time. Maybe he'll relax a little bit."

"Okay, yes, thanks, United." And then, on the other frequency, "Two Whiskey Alpha, this zero eight five heading is only five degrees off east, so just take up east on your compass. East, over."

"I read you, but I don't know what I'm doing. What is it you want me to do?"

At this point, the United captain switched his mike back to 120.4.

In the cockpit of the Mooney, the palms of the pilot's hands, his shirt, the yoke, everything seemed soaked in perspiration. "Who are all these voices that keep talking to me?" His mind had simply refused to continue to function.

"Okay, now just relax. . . ."

"Now who's that?" he thought.

"Just relax. This is United. We all get into a spot once in a while. If you just relax your hands on the wheel, just for a second, I think we'll calm down. Take your feet off the rudders and then, uh, just shake your hands for a bit and relax, and then go back to it and just head east, which is E on the indicator. East heading and, uh, hold that as steady as you can for a minute or so. Just nice and straight and I think we can calm down quite a bit and accomplish quite a bit. Okay?"

"Okay, I got yah."

"You have a good airplane under you. It's a real good machine, and, uh, with just a little help it'll do a real good job for you."

There was something so friendly, so relaxing in that slow, fatherly voice, that he felt calmer already. And, yes, suddenly he did recognize the E on the compass and seemed to succeed in holding it pretty steady.

"I'm going east now, at nine thousand."

"Very good, that's very good. Fine. Just hold that now and you'll be doing real good."

The United captain let go of the mike button, trying to figure out what to say next, when the speaker came to life again: "My gas is getting low . . . down below a quarter."

"That's all right. There's still plenty. We all make mistakes. Relax and we'll get you out of this real good."

"United, this is Oakland. Most Mooneys have a reserve of a few gallons after they go on empty—three maybe or so. We show him now forty miles two zero from Red Bluff."

"Roger. If you could work him down the valley toward Sacramento, there's lots of airports he can find to land on."

"Affirmative. Mooney two Whiskey Alpha, this is Oakland again. Continue on your present heading. It'll take another twenty miles to get you away from the mountains."

Here the captain felt a little more explanation might help. "Two Whiskey Alpha from United. Your present position is probably west of the Sacramento Valley up near Red Bluff and the center is going to take you east over the valley and then drop you down in the valley to the south where you'll have a lot better weather."

"Okay, I got yah. I hold east and keep on climbing out."

"That's right. You keep that east heading now and the people at Oakland will tell you when you're ready to descend and that'll put you in the valley. So you just listen to them and relax a little more. I think if, once in a while you just take your hands off the wheel and shake 'em a little bit and then go back, it'll be pretty easy for you. I'd set up a cruise now with your mixture leaned out so you can conserve your fuel." In order not to upset or confuse him, the captain switched again to one of the other Oakland frequencies. "Oakland, United. I'm afraid I'm going to be out of range pretty quick, so you better take it from here."

"Yes, United, and thanks."

"Good luck."

The Aztec pilot was glad the company was paying for the gas, and he was also glad to be assured that the Mooney, by now, was apparently at a safe altitude and distance from him. He had just decided to call Oakland to remind them that he was still holding and to suggest that it should now be safe for him to go on to Red Bluff, when the voice of the Mooney pilot literally screamed over the speaker.

"This is..ah . . . Whiskey Alpha. We're way out of control!"

"Oh, no! Not again!"

"Two Whiskey Alpha. This is Oakland. Let go of the controls. Release the controls, just release the controls. Let go of them. Over."

Silence.

"Two Whiskey Alpha, don't worry about the airspeed building up. Just relax. The airplane will come out of it on its own. If you're at seven thousand feet or higher, you're all right at your present position. There's clearer weather about twenty miles south. As soon as the aircraft recovers, try and take up a southerly heading."

The Aztec pilot shook his head. "If that poor sod has gotten himself in a spin, he'll never come out," he thought.

"The tank's empty!"

"If it reads empty you still have three or four gallons. We'll have to take you into Red Bluff. It's enough for that."

Why was it always, in a situation like this, that ten seconds could feel like hours?

"Two Whiskey Alpha, has the airplane righted itself? Can you tell me your airspeed?"

Somehow, the Aztec pilot was certain that he would never hear the voice of the Mooney pilot again, but he was wrong.

"My . . . ah . . . about one hundred ten miles an hour."

"If you have one-ten you're all right."

There was another long pause, then: "I'm at 5,500 and at the present time I'm going straight north, thirty-three degrees."

"You're heading toward higher terrain again. Try to turn right . . . right. Make the turn with just your rudder. Just use a little right rudder pressure, that's all, not very much, just a little. Keep your hands off the wheel—don't pull back on it or push forward. Just use a little right rudder." And then, the voice changed to a more business-like tone: "November four eight seven five Papa, Oakland."

"Seven five Pop, go ahead." Well, they hadn't forgotten him after all.

"Seven five Papa, will you give two Whiskey Alpha a call? He's about twenty-five miles north of your present position. See if you can raise him."

"Okay. Mooney two Whiskey Alpha, this is Aztec seven five Pop, do you read me, over?"

"I read you. I'm at 6,000 feet, heading . . . this thing won't stay straight."

"Okay, just steady down. I'm at 4,500 in the clear between layers, so I'm going to try and find you and take you to Red Bluff. Just try and keep a steady S on your compass and try and keep the airspeed around 110. Pull the throttle back slowly until it shows that you're coming down a little. Not too much, keep it at less than 500 feet per minute, and pretty soon you'll break out of the clouds you're in. I'm turning on my landing light, so just keep looking for a light."

The pilot had slowed the Aztec to the lowest comfortable speed, and he kept staring into the clouds to the north and above. After a while it seemed right to talk to the Mooney some more. Just as he was about to pick up the mike he caught a red flash in his peripheral vision, then another.

"Two Whiskey Alpha, I think I see you. Do you see a light straight ahead and slightly below your altitude?"

"Yes! Yes I do!"

"Seven five Pop, this is Oakland. Do you think you can lead him in?"

"Will try. Two Whiskey Alpha, this is seven five Pop. Just come on over toward me and I'll take you to Red Bluff. Oakland, five Pop, am I cleared for the approach?"

"Seven five Pop is cleared for the approach to Red Bluff Airport, Runway thirty-three. Good luck."

"Two Whiskey Alpha, I'm flying at just a little over one hundred miles an hour. Now you stay close to one side of me where I can see you. You follow me and we'll go into Red Bluff and get down."

"I'm at four thousand feet and I'm following you."

"Seven five Papa and two Whiskey Alpha, Red Bluff weather estimated ceiling eighteen hundred overcast, visibility three, light rain, altimeter two niner zero one."

"Thank you, Oakland."

"Your light seems to be disappearing. I'm losing you!"

"This is seven five Pop. Just keep on flying the way you are. We're going down through some clouds, and there'll be times when you can't see me for a few moments, but if you hold her steady the way you are, you'll be all right quite near me when we break out" *I hope!* He fed in a little extra throttle to put himself far enough ahead of the Mooney to make sure that he wouldn't suddenly run into him.

"I lost you."

"That's all right. Just keep her steady the way you're going. Just relax and keep her steady." *And now just don't mess it up in the last minute!*

"Two Whiskey Alpha, I'm now at three thousand feet and flying ninety miles an hour."

"That's good. You're doing fine. Just keep the nose down a bit and keep her coming down. I'm at twenty-five hundred, and I think I can just about see the lights of Red Bluff."

Not a word for quite a while, then, "This is two Whiskey Alpha. . . ." Just that, nothing else, then, "I can't hold it steady for some reason."

"Relax. Just steer with the rudder. Keep your hands off the wheel and maybe pull back the manifold pressure to about ten inches or so. Pretty soon you'll be breaking out of the clouds. I'm below in the clear now, and I'll wait for you here."

"I'm at twenty-five hundred feet now and about ninety miles an hour. I've got no idea what heading I've got."

"Okay, just close your throttle a little more. You're bound to be in the clear in another moment."

"I'm at about two thousand feet."

"Okay, you'll be able to see the lights on the ground in a second."

"I see 'em now."

"All right! Do you see the airport at Red Bluff? There's a rotating beacon and the runway lights are up very bright."

"Yes, I do."

Well, hallelujah! "Very good, so now just go ahead and land. Oakland Center, seven five Pop. I think I'll cancel IFR and follow the Mooney in."

"Roger, seven five Papa. Canceling IFR, and thanks for your help."

"Any time."

"This is two Whiskey Alpha. What direction am I supposed to land here?"

"I'd say it wouldn't make much difference tonight. Just pick a runway and land on it. I'll give 'em a call and tell 'em you're coming."

"This is Oakland. Red Bluff reports they have him in sight."

"Okay, I guess he got away with it, then."

"Can you see him landing?"

"I'm not sure."

"This is two Whiskey Alpha. I'm having trouble with my landing gear now."

Oh no! Not now! "Is that the kind of Mooney with the gear with the long handle?"

"Yes."

"Well, put the handle all the way down again and then try once more in one quick, smooth motion, and it'll just slip into the catch under the instrument panel."

"Ah, I got it."

"Good."

"I'm going to land to the north."

"That's just fine."

"This is Oakland. How's he doing?"

"Fine. He's got his landing lights on and . . . okay, he's on the ground and slowing down."

"Then he made it?"

"We all did. Don't ask me how. Good night, gentlemen."

* * *

This story is based on fact. Many of the communications, particularly the voice of the Mooney pilot during periods of stress, were taken from the transcript of the recordings that were made at Oakland Center and the Red Bluff FSS. Aircraft identifications were changed to protect those involved.

The incident is presented here to illustrate what the onset of panic can do to a pilot and to show how much help is available if a pilot will only ask for it.

20
Westchester County to Boston

THROUGHOUT THE DRIVE FROM NEW YORK CITY TO THE WESTCHESTER County Airport, the pilot kept looking at the sky, wondering if he'd be able to take off safely. According to the information he had obtained by telephone, the airport was still IFR, but was expected to go VFR some time during the morning. His destination, Boston, on the other hand, was VFR, but there was some weather coming down from Canada that indicated it might just turn sour later in the day. With Boston's Logan Airport being one where special VFR operations were not permitted, he might have difficulty getting in there if he had to wait too long for Westchester County to clear.

When he got to the airport, it was still IFR with an 800-foot ceiling and visibility less than 1 mile, which put it below minimums for a special VFR takeoff. He asked about reports on the tops of the overcast and was told that they had been reported at 5,000 feet.

He now held a little discussion with himself. Even though he did not hold an IFR ticket, he felt completely confident that he could climb safely to VFR conditions on top. The only trouble was that he thought he might sound less than professional if he should go ahead and ask for an IFR clearance. On the other hand, if he didn't get out of there soon, he might never be able to get to Boston in the near future—and getting there was important.

HE MADE UP HIS MIND

Finally, he reached his decision. He called Flight Service and filed an IFR flight plan to VFR conditions on top and then direct to Boston. He preflighted his airplane, fired up the engine, and called ground control for his clearance, hoping rather desperately that ATC wouldn't foul him up with some kind of complicated instructions.

Pencil and pad in hand, just in case, he waited. He was lucky. The clearance simply read, "Cleared as filed," plus a transponder code and departure control frequency, both of which he jotted down and read back easily. Then, while taxiing to the end of the runway, he set the transponder to the required code and tuned his number two com to the departure frequency and his number one to the tower.

It's uncomfortable to sit at the end of the runway when the visibility is such that one can't see the other end. Still, he was familiar with the airport and its surroundings, so he figured he would be able to take off and climb to a safe altitude without getting into any trouble.

"Ready to go."

"Cleared for takeoff."

He accelerated down the runway, lifted off, and moments later was in the soup.

"Contact departure control."

He did, was told that he was in radar contact, and continued his climbout by instruments, careful not to take his eyes off the instruments so as not to get bothered or confused by the masses of gray clouds rushing by his windows on either side. It didn't take long—although it seemed as if it did—until things got lighter above, and moments later he broke out into brilliant sunshine above a solid undercast. He leveled off at 7,500 feet and called departure control and canceled IFR.

"Roger, canceling IFR."

He was on his own, and he breathed a sigh of relief. It had been the first time he had actually filed IFR, and he'd gotten away with it. He called Hartford for the latest Boston weather and found that it was down to 3,000 broken and 3 miles in haze. Well, if it stayed that way he'd be able to make it all right. He'd be able to get down VFR through breaks in the overcast and if the visibility held, a VFR approach and landing would be legal. But what if it got worse? Well, he'd simply have to wait and see. After all, if all else failed, he had sufficient fuel to get back to New York, which according to the forecasts, was supposed to be VFR by afternoon.

Anyway, it wasn't the first time that he had been VFR on top with no clear idea whether or not he'd be able to get down at his destination. It had always worked before, so why shouldn't it today?

He was tuned to the Putnam VOR, which is remoted from Worcester, when it was time for the hourly weather sequence, and this time the report for Boston was not what he had hoped to hear: 3,000 overcast, visibility 2. Not only wouldn't he be able to get down through the solid overcast—even if he could, he wouldn't be able to land at Logan without an IFR clearance. And one of those in one day was about all he was prepared to handle.

What about the other three airports in the area? There was Norwood, Hanscom, and Beverly, and they would have to give him a special VFR clearance if he asked for it, assuming, of course, that he could somehow find a way down through the overcast.

He continued on at 7,500 feet, which would keep him above the Boston TCA, and decided to fly to the vicinity of each of the secondary airports to see if he could locate some breaks in the overcast. He vaguely remembered that the weather sequence had included a report of broken conditions for Worcester, so he figured that if worse came to worst, he could land there and rent a car for the 35 or so miles into Boston.

It took a while, but everything underneath remained a solid mass of clouds. Apparently there was no chance in the immediate vicinity of Boston to get down unless he was willing to simply drop through the clouds. Somehow, he didn't feel comfortable with that idea despite the reported 3,000-foot ceiling. He was certain that he could have made it if he had to, but he just didn't feel good with the thought.

He tuned his nav receivers to the 010-degree radial from Putnam, which should take him right on top of the Worcester airport. Then he called Worcester for the current weather and was given 1,500 scattered, 4,000 overcast, visibility 5. Breaks in the overcast to the north, so that place was going down, too. He'd better hurry.

THE CLOUDS WERE SOLID

When he finally arrived over Worcester, the clouds were solid, so he turned north to look for the reported breaks. He'd been heading that way for maybe five or six minutes when, off to the right, he spotted something that looked as if it might be a break.

He turned toward it, and once he got there, he saw something that looked like water and a bit of shore. He checked his chart and decided that what he was looking at

Fig. 20-1. *Then he was in the clear again. . . .*

must be the Wachusett Reservoir. Fine. Granted, there was a 2,049-foot broadcast tower indicated just to the southeast of the reservoir, but as long as he stayed over the water he would be safe.

He trimmed his airplane to a reasonable rate of descent and started to circle down through the open space, constantly keeping the water beneath in view.

Suddenly, he found himself in the clouds, but only for a second or two. Then he was in the clear again, and although the visibility wasn't much, he saw that all the clouds were now above him (FIG. 20-1). He leveled off, took up a southwesterly heading, and called Worcester Tower to announce his imminent arrival.

He rented a car, drove to Boston, took care of his business there, stayed overnight, returned to Worcester the next day in bright sunshine, and flew back legally VFR all the way.

21
Running out of VFR

WHAT FOLLOWS IS A CLASSIC CASE OF ATTEMPTED VFR FLIGHT UNDER exceedingly marginal conditions by a crew unprepared for such an operation. The event is related in its entirety in the form of a conversation between the pilot and copilot, a transcript of which was provided by the National Transportation Safety Board. Although the airplane involved was an airliner—a Convair 600 turboprop—and the crew was instrument rated, it does serve to illustrate dramatically how even experienced pilots can get themselves into trouble.

Although there is no record of it, it must be assumed that the decision by the crew to forego the usual IFR clearance and to proceed VFR was based on the reports of a line of thunderstorms lying across their route and the assumption that it would be more expedient and possibly safer to deal with them by staying in VFR conditions, despite the fact that the flight was to take place after dark.

The aircraft was equipped with a cockpit voice recorder, which yielded the following conversation. Note that there are indications that the crew did not have any Sectional or WAC charts for the area in the cockpit, and thus they had no clear idea of the terrain.

One of the many lessons to be learned from this case is that VFR flight under marginal weather conditions should never be attempted unless WAC—or, preferably, Sectional—charts are available.

SHORTLY AFTER TAKEOFF

The recording started shortly after the Convair took off. "That might not be a hole there," said the captain.

"We'll know shortly. It sorta looks like twenty-four miles to the end. I don't mind, do you?" the copilot asked.

"I don't care, just as long as we don't go through it."

"Looks a little strange through there. Looks like something attenuating through there."

"It's a shadow."

"Yeah, looks like a shadow."

"Is that better?"

"Naw, I don't care."

"Suit yourself."

"Well, I don't know, looks a little lighter in here. This thing hits your eyeballs pretty hard."

"That's right."

After a short period of time, the captain said, "See something?"

"I still think it's a shadow," the copilot answered.

"Yeah, why not?"

"I'd slow up a bit, too."

"What have we got, decreasing ground pickup?"

"I didn't hear you."

"The visibility is dropping." Then, "Rain!"

"Raining all over the place."

And some minutes later, "What's all this? Are those lights in those fields? What are they, chicken farms?"

"Yeah."

"Gosh almighty, they're planning to grow a few eggs, ain't they?"

"That's what they are."

And later still, "There's not much to that but we've got to stay away from it or we'll be IFR."

"Shoot, I can't get this stupid radar. Got any idea where we're at?"

"Yeah. Two one six will take us right to the VOR."

"Two . . . ah. . . ."

"Two oh one, I've got."

"Fifteen."

"I'm not concerned with that," the captain said. "I couldn't care less. I guess you're right. That is just extending on and on as we go along because it hasn't moved in about three or four miles in the last thirty minutes, it seems like. I guess it's building up that way now." After a moment, "What's Hot Springs'?"

"Sir?"

"What's Hot Springs' VOR? It is ten-zero, is that right?"

"Yeah, yeah, that's right. We don't want to get too far up the . . . it gets hilly."

"Yeah. Stars are shining. Why don't you try two thousand? If we get up here anywhere near Hot Springs, we get in the mountains."

"Uh, you reckon there's a ridge line along here somewhere? Go down five hundred feet, you can see all kinds of lights. Let's go ahead and try for twenty-five hundred."

After apparently having climbed to a somewhat higher altitude, "All right, Fred, you can quit worrying about the mountains because that'll clear everything over here."

"That's why I wanted to go to twenty-five hundred feet. That's the Hot Springs highway right here, I think."

"You're about right."

"Texarkana . . . no, it ain't either. Texarkana's back here."

"Texarkana's back over here someplace."

"Yeah. This ain't no Hot Springs highway."

By now the flight is 18 minutes and 34 seconds old.

"Well, thirty degrees . . . thirty degrees takes you right to Texarkana, doesn't it? Hot Springs . . . here we're sitting on fifty."

Yeah. How're we doing on the ground?"

"I don't know, Fred. Still keep getting another one popping up every time . . . every time."

"If we keep this up indefinitely, we'll be in Tulsa."

"I haven't been in Tulsa in years."

"Ha ha. The last time, I was with Glen Duke. He said, 'Go whichever way you want to.' I was going out of Abilene going to Dallas. Took up a heading of zero-one-zero and flew for about 45 minutes and he said, 'Fred, you can't keep going on this heading.' I said, 'Why?' He said, 'You're gonna be in Oklahoma pretty soon.' I said, I said, 'I don't care if I'm in Oklahoma.' He said, 'Fair enough.' "

And then, after a moment, "How'd I get all this speed?"

"You're all right."

"Pile it on? We'll keep this speed here?"

"A little while."

"There ain't no lights on the ground over there." (FIG. 21-1)

"Yeah. I see 'em behind us. See stars above us."

"I got some lights on the ground."

"There's just not many out there."

"Maybe . . . could be something else, coach."

"Ah, we're getting rid of the clouds!" And a few seconds later, "We is in the clouds, Fred."

"Are we?"

"Yeah . . . no, we're not. I can see above us."

"We got ground up ahead?"

"I can see the ground here."

"Yeah, I can see the ground down here, too."

Fig. 21-1. *"There ain't no lights on the ground over there."*

"I can see some lights over here."

"That's probably Hot Springs, coach."

"Yep, could be. Yeah, that might be either it or Arkadelphia."

"Well, I'm getting out of the clouds here, but then I'm getting right straight into it."

"Oh, looks like you're all right."

"Do you see any stars above us? We're getting in and out of some scud." (FIG. 21-2)

"Yeah, we've got a little bit here."

"I sure wish I knew where we were."

"Well, I'll tell you what, we're ah . . . on the two fifty, two sixty radial from, ah . . . Hot Springs."

LITTLE SUCCESS WITH RADAR

The copilot was trying, apparently with little success, to use the airborne weather radar.

Fig. 21-2. *"We're getting in and out of some scud."*

"Painting ridges and everything else, boss, and I'm not familiar with the terrain."
Then, "We're staying in the clouds."

"Yeah, I'd stay down. You're right in the base of the clouds. I'll tell you what.
We're going to be able to turn here in a minute."

"You wanna go through there?"

"Yeah."

"All right. Good. Looking good, looking good."

"That's all right. Wait a minute."

"Well, I can't even get Texarkana any more."

"I'll tell you what, Fred."

" 'Kay, boss."

"Well, ah . . . we'll just try that. We'll try it. We're gonna be in the rain pretty
soon. It's only about two miles wide."

"You tell me where you want me to go."

"Okay, give me a heading of, ah . . . two ninety."

"Two ninety."

"You got six miles to turn."

"We're in it."

"Huh?"

"We're in solid now."

"Are we?"

"Hold it."

"Start your turn . . . standard rate . . . level out and let me see it when you hit two ninety."

"Ah, okay." After a moment, "There's your two ninety."

"Steady on. Should hit in about half a mile. Should be out of it in about two miles . . . you're in it . . . are you through it?" In another moment, "Turn thirty left."

"I can see the ground now. There's thirty. Naw, that's thirty-five."

"Keep on truckin', just keep on truckin'."

"Well, we must be somewhere in Oklahoma."

"Doing all the good in the world."

"Do you have any idea of what the frequency of the Paris VOR is?"

"Nope, I don't really give a darn. Put, ah . . . about two sixty five heading . . . two sixty five."

"Fred, descent to two thousand."

"Two thousand coming up." Then, "Here we are, we're not out of it."

Fig. 21-3. *"The highest point around here is about 1,200 feet."*

"Let's truck on."

"Right."

"That's all right. You're doing all the good in the world. I thought we'd get . . . thought it was moving that way on me, only we kinda turned a little bit while you was looking at the map."

"First time I ever made a mistake in my life."

"I'll be, man, I wish I knew where we were so we'd have some idea of the general terrain around this place."

"I know what it is."

"What?"

"The highest point out here is about twelve hundred feet." (FIG. 21-3)

"That right?"

"The whole general area, and then we're not even sure where that is, I don't believe."

"I'll tell you what, as long as we travel northwest instead of west, I still can't get Paris." A little later, "We're about to pass over the Page VOR. You know where that is?"

"Yeah."

"All right."

"About a hundred and eighty degrees to Texarkana."

"About one fifty-two . . . the minimum en route altitude around here is forty-four hun. . . ."

The recording ended with the sound of an impact, 33 minutes and 41 seconds into the flight.

22
An Instrument Rating?

MANY A NOVICE PILOT READING THIS BOOK WILL UNDOUBTEDLY SAY TO himself with complete conviction, "No matter how much and how long I fly, I will never get myself into the kinds of situations that have been described in this book." And, for a while, at least, he might actually succeed in avoiding all those marginal conditions.

Gradually, however, as time begins to pile up in his logbook, along with the self-assurance of his ability, his attitude toward what he considered marginal will inexorably change. He will learn to accept and deal with gradually increasing crosswind components during takeoffs and landings; he will take off and fly when it's raining and when the overcast is barely above VFR minimums; and he will climb into VFR conditions on top when he finds breaks in the clouds that permit him to maintain visual contact with the ground. Eventually, he will find himself confronted with the kind of conditions he had earlier decided to avoid at all cost.

The fact is, if you want to make sufficient use of the airplane to justify your investment in it and the cost of flight training, you have to do a lot of flying, and that just isn't always possible if you restrict your activity to CAVU days.

The question that naturally comes to mind is, should you get an instrument rating? The answer must necessarily be a qualified "yes."

The trouble is that instrument ratings are not only expensive, but difficult to obtain. Once a pilot is instrument-rated, it takes a lot of continuous practice to remain sufficiently proficient to be able to use it safely when the need arises.

Different pilots have different attitudes toward instrument ratings. There are those who simply say, "Who needs it?" They might have started flying during the time when airspace was truly free, when the concept of air traffic control was just a gleam in the eye of some executive of the infant airline industry.

I know more than a few pilots, whose names most aviators would recognize immediately, who are holdovers from those days. One in particular has thousands of hours in literally dozens of airplane types, but has never seen the need to get an instrument rating. (In fact, he might be the only regular pilot of a jet aircraft in the United States who cannot legally fly on instruments.) Another, who is the author of dozens of books on flying safety, stubbornly refuses to get an instrument endorsement.

These pilots and others are probably excellent pilots, but in terms of today's use of airspace, they must be considered relics who don't fit in any longer.

Then there are those who keep saying to themselves that they'll do it one of these days, but time passes and they continue to successfully squeak by, staying more or less VFR, and the urgency and desire to be instrument-rated gradually recedes until it becomes one of those things you always wanted to do but never got around to.

Akin to the procrastinator is the pilot who justifies not getting instrument training by pointing out that if he was rated, he might be tempted to fly in bad weather, and as everyone knows, bad weather is the cause of more accidents than any other source.

The real reason that many do not get the rating is that they simply cannot afford the cost or time involved in going through the rigorous training involved.

Another category is the pilot who actually took all the required training but flunked the written test. The written is difficult, and much of it consists of subjects that might prove to be of little value later.

Many of us, once our school and college years are behind us by a decade or so, find it extremely difficult to readjust our attitude and thinking toward cramming for an exam. Educators are discovering what most of us have known for years—that we are not created equal in our ability to learn. Some of us learn more quickly through visual orientation, while others assimilate better from aural presentations. Many of us utilize parts of both methods.

In any case, once having flunked the test, you might be tempted to decide that you know enough about instrument flying in order to use it when the occasion arises and that, therefore, it isn't worth the effort (and possibly the embarrassment) to try to take the test again.

TWO BASIC CATEGORIES

Instrument-rated pilots, too, fall into two basic categories. There are those who obtained their rating and use it constantly. They will fly instruments even when the weather is VFR and virtually every approach to a landing becomes a practice instrument approach. These pilots become and remain proficient, and they learn to recognize their own limitations as pilots in terms of performance, as well as the limits of the available equipment of the aircraft they are flying. But, excluding the professionals flying for the airlines, corporations, or air-charter services, their number is most probably in the minority.

A vast number of instrument-rated pilots are businessmen who use their aircraft in their profession. Initially, after they obtained their rating, they might have used it with some degree of frequency. But as time passed, they found more often than not that it is simpler and quicker to operate VFR. Consequently, they gradually used the instrument ticket less and less often. When they did use it, it was probably just to climb through an overcast to VFR conditions on top or to descend through an undercast to an airport where the ceiling was 1,000 feet or better and the visibility ample.

However, there always comes that day when you simply feel that you have to be at a certain place although the conditions are barely above IFR minimums. Then the psychological attitude that results from having an instrument rating and therefore being in a position to legally make that approach will influence you and you will try to make that VOR or ADF approach to that airport where you have never been before. Most of the time you'll probably make it, but then there might always be that one time when you don't.

The trouble is that for the average general aviation pilot making nonprecision and even precision approaches under minimum or near-minimum conditions, it is a lot harder than it is for our airline counterparts. They operate with two- or three-pilot crews, flying aircraft equipped with every conceivable electronic aid (most of them in duplicate or triplicate), and they nearly always fly into airports where they have been hundreds of times before. We, on the other hand, are usually alone in the cockpit, often fly to unfamiliar airports, and must deal with much less sophisticated instrumentation.

There are those who claim, with considerable justification, that no single pilot should attempt to fly a tight instrument approach in an airplane that is not equipped with a reliable autopilot. The pilot workload involved in communicating with ATC, studying approach charts, and at the same time flying the airplane, usually in turbulence, is just too much to be handled safely by one person.

The question still remains: Should every serious pilot attempt to become instrument-rated? There is no hard and fast answer. One consideration is money. If finances permit undertaking the expense not only of the flight training involved, but also of obtaining the kind of instrumentation for the airplane that will turn it into an efficient and safe instrument ship, then by all means, the rating should be obtained.

There can be no question that instrument training makes us better pilots, as long as we continue to be careful not to fall prey to overconfidence. This type of training, more than any other, teaches us to always stay ahead of the airplane and to be comfortable with it when it and its instruments are the only things that stand between life and death.

THE WRITTEN EXAM

If passing the written seems too troublesome, there are a number of organizations around the country that specialize in "cram" courses. They usually involve just one weekend of continuous lectures and study, culminating in the exam on Monday. Most of these organizations will guarantee that you pass the exam, meaning that if you fail, you can retake the course and the exam free of charge as often as necessary to eventually pass.

Note that these courses don't actually teach much. All they are designed to do is to get the student over the hurdle of the pesky written. Pilots contemplating obtaining an instrument rating might be best advised to take one of these cram courses first, and thus get the written out of the way. They can then clear their heads of all that extraneous junk that is part of the written and concentrate on the flight portion of the training, which is where actual instrument flying is being learned.

If money is a problem, if the best you can do is to take an instrument flight lesson every week or two, it might not be worth it at all. Instrument training requires a great deal of concentration. There is much to be learned and to be remembered, and when such training is squeezed in between the day-to-day routine of running a business or efficiently performing some type of job, you might not have enough energy left to absorb all the information the instructor will be trying to convey.

WHICH HALF SHOULD YOU BELONG TO?

Of the total number of pilots in the United States, nearly half are instrument-rated. If you're in the other half, it's nothing about which you should be embarrassed. As long as you remain aware of the limitations of your capabilities and the performance limitations of the airplanes you fly, you will be able to operate safely most of the time.

Never forget that, regardless of what part of the country you're talking about (with the possible exception of the Aleutians and parts of Alaska), the weather is good much more often than it is bad. If you are willing to accept the fact that there are times when you simply can't fly or can't get to where you wanted to go, then there's no reason why the lack of an instrument rating should present any serious problem.

Glossary

ADF—Abbreviation for Automatic Direction Finder.

agl—Abbreviation for above ground level.

AIM—Acronym for Airman's Information Manual.

airport advisory area—The area within 10 nautical miles of an airport without an operational control tower and on which a Flight Service Station is located.

airport advisory service—An information service provided by Flight Service Stations at airports not served by a control tower.

Airport Radar Service Area (ARSA)—An area in which all pilots are required to establish radio contact with ATC and abide by its instructions.

airport traffic area—A circular area, 10 nautical miles in diameter, surrounding a controlled airport, including the airspace from the ground up to, but not including, 3,000 feet agl. When operating within this airspace, aircraft must maintain radio contact with that airport's control tower.

APU—Abbreviation for Auxiliary Power Unit.

artificial horizon—An air-data instrument that shows the relation of the attitude of the aircraft to the horizon.

ATC—Abbreviation for Air Traffic Control.

ATIS—Abbreviation for Automatic Terminal Information Service, continually broadcast recorded information about airport conditions.

BFR—Abbreviation for Biennial Flight Review.

C—Abbreviation for the centigrade (or Celsius) temperature scale.

CAT—Acronym for Clear Air Turbulence.

CAVU—Acronym for Ceiling And Visibility Unlimited.

compass rose—A circle, graduated in degrees, printed on some charts or marked on the ground at an airport and used as a reference to either true or magnetic direction.

CDI—Abbreviation for Course-Deviation Indicator.

CDU—Abbreviation for Control-Display Unit.

ceiling—Broken or overcast cloud cover that obscures 60 percent or more of the sky.

com radio—Shortened form of communication radio.

control-display unit—The panel-mounted display that provides the interface between the pilot and the area navigation computer.

controlled airport—Any airport with an operating control tower.

controlled airspace—Airspace within which IFR traffic must maintain contact with ATC.

control zone—The area around a controlled airport, normally approximately circular in shape and extending five nautical miles in all directions, plus any extensions necessary for instrument approaches and departures, under active ATC control. It extends upward from the ground to the base of the Continental Control Area, or, where not underlying the Continental Control Area, it has no upper limit.

density altitude—Pressure altitude corrected for temperature variations.

DG—Abbreviation for Directional Gyro.

directional gyro—A gyroscopic compass that must be reset periodically to conform with the magnetic compass.

DME—Abbreviation for Distance Measuring Equipment.

EAA—Abbreviation for Experimental Aircraft Association.

EGT—Abbreviation for Exhaust Gas Temperature gauge.

E6b—A mechanical hand-held flight computer, similar in operation to a slide rule.

ETA—Abbreviation for Estimated Time of Arrival.

F—Abbreviation for the Fahrenheit temperature scale.

FARs—Acronym for Federal Air Regulations.

FBO—Abbreviation for Fixed-Base Operator.

fpm—Abbreviation for feet per minute.

FSS—Abbreviation for Flight Service Station.

GS—Abbreviation for Glide Slope, either visual or electronic, that provides vertical guidance during approach and landing.

GMT—Abbreviation for Greenwich Mean Time, or Zulu Time.

HSI—Abbreviation for Horizontal Situation Indicator.

IAS—Abbreviation for Indicated AirSpeed.

ident—Shortened form of Identification; also a controller's request for a pilot to activate the transponder identification feature to help confirm an aircraft's identity.

IFR—Abbreviation for Instrument Flight Rules, rules governing operation in below-minimum visual flight conditions.

ILS—Abbreviation for Instrument Landing System.

Jepp charts—Shortened form of Jeppesen charts, radio facility charts produced and marketed by Jeppesen-Sanderson.

kHz—Abbreviation for kiloHertz, a measure equal to 1,000 cycles.

knots—Nautical miles per hour, abbreviated kts.

LMM—Compass locator at middle marker on ILS.

localizer—The horizontal guidance portion of an ILS.

LOM—A compass locator colocated with the outer marker.

Loran C—A low-frequency navigation system using specialized ground-based transmitters to determine an airplane's position in terms of longitude and latitude.

MEA—Abbreviation for Minimum En route Altitude.

MHz—Abbreviation for MegaHertz, a measure equal to 1 million cycles.

MLS—Abbreviation for Microwave Landing System.

MM—Middle Marker on the ILS system.

mph—Statute miles per hour.

msl—Height above mean sea level in feet.

nav aid—A ground-based station equipped with electronic navigation aids, such as a VOR or NDB.

nav receiver—A radio receiver designed to receive signals from ground-based nav aids.

NDB—Abbreviation for Non-Directional Beacon.

nm—Abbreviation for nautical miles.

Notam—Shortened form of Notice to Airmen, notices published periodically by the FAA.

OBI—Abbreviation for Omni-Bearing Indicator, a panel-mounted instrument that displays information received by the VHF nav receiver.

OBS—Abbreviation for Omni-Bearing Selector, the knob on the OBI that permits selection of a given radial or bearing from or to a VOR station.

OM—Outer Marker on the ILS system.

pilotage—Flying solely by reference to visual ground-based landmarks.

PIREPs—Voluntary pilot reports of conditions.

RNAV—Shortened form of area navigation.

rpm—Abbreviation for revolutions per minute.

Sectional—An aviation chart with a scale of 1″ = 500,000′ that includes, among other information, terrain features. It is the preferred type of chart for VFR flight.

service ceiling—The altitude at which an aircraft can climb at a maximum of 100 fpm; usually referenced at gross weight and Standard Day conditions.

sm—Abbreviation for statute miles.

SVFR—Abbreviation for Special VFR.

TAS—Abbreviation for True AirSpeed.

TCA—Abbreviation for Terminal Control Area.

transponder—A panel-mounted electronic pulse instrument that enhances the aircraft's radar return on controller screens.

transponder code—The frequency channel to which the transponder is tuned. ATC will request that the pilot tune his transponder to a given code with the phrase: "Squawk zero one hundred" or some other number.

TRSA —Abbreviation for Terminal Radar Service Area.

turn-and-bank indicator—Also known as needle-and-ball, a basic cockpit instrument that shows the attitude of the wings relative to the horizontal plane and the correct use of rudder during turns.

uncontrolled airspace—Airspace in which VFR minimums are less than those in controlled airspace and in which IFR traffic may operate under instrument conditions without being in contact with ATC, which has no jurisdiction over this space.

Unicom—A radio facility normally found at uncontrolled airports or FBOs that is used to transmit or obtain unofficial information.

VASI—Abbreviation for Visual Approach Slope Indicator, a glide slope system that uses a series of lights to indicate the correct vertical angle for landing.

Vertical Speed Indicator (VSI)—An air-data instrument showing the rate of climb or descent.

VFR—Abbreviation for Visual Flight Rules or the weather conditions under which VFR traffic may operate.

VHF—Abbreviation for Very High Frequency.

Victor Airways—Aerial "highways" in airspace below 18,000 feet msl that are flight lanes between VORs.

VOR—Abbreviation for Very high frequency Omni-directional Radio range, a ground-based nav aid that is the primary means of radio navigation in the United States.

VORDME—A VOR colocated with a DME facility.

VORTAC—A VOR colocated with a Tactical Air Navigation (TACAN) facility. For all practical purposes the same as a VORDME.

VSI—Abbreviation for Vertical Speed Indicator, or rate of climb indicator.

WAC—Acronym for World Aeronautical Chart, similar to a Sectional but in half its scale (1″ = 1,000,000′).

waypoint—A phantom VOR artificially created through the use of RNAV equipment.

W/P or WP—Abbreviation for WayPoint.

yoke—Control wheel.

Zulu time—Greenwich Mean Time.

Index

turbulence, 43-48, 57, 171, 172
  flying above, 160-161
turn-and-bank indicator, 93
turns, 95-96

U

uncontrolled airspace, 9
unusual attitudes, 95

V

vertical speed indicator (VSI), 6, 93
VFR
  above clouds, 9-15
  running out of, 187-193
  Special (S/VFR), 23-29
VHF nav receivers, 99-105
visibility, 19-32
visible moisture, 68
visual flight rules (VFR), ix

VOR, 107, 108, 113, 119, 120, 121
VOR/DME, 107, 108
VORTAC, 107, 108, 113, 114

W

wake turbulence, 46-48
warm front, 59, 60
waypoint (W/P), 113, 117
weather
  charts, 64-66
  fronts, 59-64
  mountain flying, 54-55
  winter, 84-85
weight, 125-127
wind, 33-42
  mountain flying, 55
wind shear, 41, 74
wing levelers, 122-123
winter flying, 83-87

Other Bestsellers of Related Interest

ABCs OF SAFE FLYING—2nd Edition
—David Frazier

Attitude, basics, and communication are the ABCs David Frazier talks about in this revised second edition of a book that answers all the obvious questions, and reminds you of others you might forget to ask. This edition includes additional advanced flight maneuvers, and a clear explanation of the Federal Airspace system. 198 pages, 69 illustrations. Book No. 2430, $12.95 paperback only

IMPROVE YOUR FLYING SKILLS: Tips from a Pro—Donald J. Clausing

Learn firsthand the professional attitudes, flying standards, and everyday procedures practiced by airline and corporate aircraft captains. Leading off with an overview of the basics of flying VFR and IFR, the author gives in-depth coverage of all the things that make up advanced, no-nonsense airmanship. Among the topics covered: flight planning, cruise control, types of approaches, weather flying, filing IFR, radio procedures and "BILAHs" (Briefing, IFR, Log, Alternate, Hazardous weather). 224 pages, 42 illustrations. Book No. 3328, $14.95 paperback, $24.95 hardcover

THE JOY OF FLYING—2nd Edition—Robert Mark

Here are the answers to just about every question a nonflyer could have about flying. From practical information to humorous sidelights, Mark covers what it's like to be behind the controls of an aircraft, the ins and outs of pilot training, techniques for communicating with air traffic control, reasons and requirements for advanced pilot ratings, even the ten greatest lies to tell a nonflying spouse. It's a fascinating and fun-filled look at the pleasures, challenges, and requirements of learning to pilot an airplane. 176 pages, 67 illustrations. Book No. 2444, $14.95 paperback only

The classic you've been searching for . . .
STICK AND RUDDER: An Explanation of the Art of Flying—Wolfgang Langewiesche

Students, certificated pilots, and instructors alike have praised this book as *"the most useful guide to flying ever written."* The book explains the important phases of the art of flying, in a way the learner can use. It shows precisely what the pilot does when he flies, just how he does it, and why. 395 pages, illustrated. Book No. 3820, $18.95 hardcover only

BECOMING AN AIRLINE PILOT—Jeff Griffin

Discover exactly what it takes to pursue a cockpit career, from the basics of flight school to your probationary year as a commercial pilot. This is a down-to-earth look at what really goes into preparing for and landing a job with a civilian career. You'll learn why it's important to start aiming at that career goal as early as your mid-teens. Griffin tells you how to write a resume and cover letter, how and where to send them, plus many more helpful job-hunting tips. 128 pages, 38 illustrations. Book No. 2449, $12.95 paperback only

THE ILLUSTRATED GUIDE TO AERODYNAMICS—Hubert "Skip" Smith

If you've always considered aerodynamic science a highly technical area best left to professional engineers and aircraft designers . . . this outstanding new sourcebook will change your mind! Smith introduces the principles of aerodynamics to everyone who wants to know how and why aircraft fly . . . but who doesn't want to delve into exotic theories or complicated mathematical relationships. 240 pages, 232 illustrations. Book No. 2390, $17.95 paperback only

FLYING IN CONGESTED AIRSPACE: A Private Pilot's Guide—Kevin Garrison

This book examines the problems and concerns of flying in congested airspace and focuses on how general aviation pilots can best deal with them. It's so complete, it can be used as a primer for operating at the 11 busiest terminals in the U.S. 224 pages, 74 illustrations. Book No. 2446, $16.95 paperback, $24.95 hardcover

THE PILOT'S RADIO COMMUNICATIONS HANDBOOK—3rd Edition
—Paul E. Illman and Jay Pouzar
". . . should have a spot on your bookshelf . . ."
                                        —*Private Pilot*
". . . time spent on this book is sure to make your flight smoother."   —*Kitplanes*

An updated edition of a popular handbook, this guide contains information on FAA rule changes regarding Mode C transponders, single-class TCA operations, and student pilot TCA training requirements. Current issues relating to the entire spectrum of VFR radio communications are addressed. Now, you can use even the busiest airports with confidence and skill. 240 pages, 61 illustrations. Book No. 2445, $15.95 paperback only

MASTERING INSTRUMENT FLYING
—Henry Sollman with Sherwood Harris

Mastering Instrument Flying introduces an entirely new course designed from beginning to end to meet or exceed the Instrument Flight Test standards recently published by the FAA. The elements, techniques, procedures, and tolerances of instrument flight are addressed in precise detail. Illustrated information on how to prepare for the instrument flight test is provided, and additional advanced procedures not specifically required for the instrument rating are covered. 336 pages, 256 illustrations. Book No. 2433, $18.95 paperback only

GENERAL AVIATION LAW—Jerry A. Eichenberger

Although the regulatory burden that is part of flying sometimes seems overwhelming, it need not take the pleasure out of your flight time. Eichenberger provides an up-to-date survey of many aviation regulations, and gives you a solid understanding of FAA procedures and functions, airman ratings and maintenance certificates, the implications of aircraft ownership, and more. This book allows you to recognize legal problems before they result in FAA investigations and the potentially serious consequences. 240 pages. Book No. 3431, $16.95 paperback, $25.95 hardcover

THE ART OF INSTRUMENT FLYING
—2nd Edition—J. R. Williams

". . . as complete and up-to-date as an instrument book can be." —*Aero Magazine*

Williams has updated his comprehensive guide to include flight director, Loran-C, and Omega navigational systems: en route, area, TCA, and SID/STAR reference charts reflect current designations. The book addresses all elements of IFR flight. The first edition won the 1989 Best Technical Book award of the Western Region of the Aviation/Space Writers Association. 352 pages, 113 illustrations. Book No. 3654, $19.95 paperback, $31.95 hardcover

THE PILOT'S GUIDE TO WEATHER REPORTS, FORECASTS & FLIGHT PLANNING
—Terry T. Lankford

This comprehensive guide to aviation weather for all pilots offers clear explanations, real-life examples, and effective illustrations. It shows you how to access weather services efficiently, translate briefings correctly, and apply reports and forecasts to specific preflight and in-flight situations to expand your margin of safety. 397 pages, 123 illustrations. Book No. 3582, $19.95 paperback, $29.95 hardcover

Look for These and Other TAB Books at Your Local Bookstore

To Order Call Toll Free 1-800-822-8158

(in PA, AK, and Canada call 717-794-2191)

or write to TAB Books, Blue Ridge Summit, PA 17294-0840.

Title	Product No.	Quantity	Price

☐ Check or money order made payable to TAB Books

Charge my ☐ VISA ☐ MasterCard ☐ American Express

Acct. No. _____ Exp. _____

Signature: _____

Name: _____

Address: _____

City: _____

State: _____ Zip: _____

Subtotal $ _____

Postage and Handling
($3.00 in U.S., $5.00 outside U.S.) $ _____

Add applicable state and local
sales tax $ _____

TOTAL $ _____

TAB Books catalog free with purchase; otherwise send $1.00 in check
or money order and receive $1.00 credit on your next purchase.

Orders outside U.S. must pay with international money order in U.S. dollars.

**TAB Guarantee: If for any reason you are not satisfied with the book(s)
you order, simply return it (them) within 15 days and receive a full
refund.**
BC